The Cure for Stupidity

If you're like me, a believer of expanding human potential, then Eric Bailey has your back. *The Cure for Stupidity* is all about helping leaders and managers understand their teams so that they can be the best they can be.

–Derek Muller, PhD, Creator of Veritasium on YouTube

Teamwork is the key to increasing your competitive advantage in combat and the corporate world. To build a high performing team of humans, you need to first understand human perceptions and misperceptions, then relearn how to communicate with each other, and ultimately, create a shared understanding to align your action and daily decision making. This is tough but important work. Thankfully, Eric Bailey's "Principles of Human Understanding" form an incredibly useful guidebook. He shared these principles with our leadership teams, taught us how to think better and feel deeper, and grew our ability to build the future of Airpower! In a fun, yet powerful way, this book tells us something we all need to hear—that to win, we need to listen and think differently!

–Brigadier General Brook J. Leonard, USAF

The Cure for Stupidity is a must-read for any leader, individual, or team looking to reduce friction and accelerate. The content will help you change not only your own methods of communication, but also how you view and understand those around you. The principles that Eric Bailey outlines in his book can change how the world communicates!

–Nicole Lance, MPA, Founder of Arizona Women Leading Government

Pick up a copy of Eric's new book, *The Cure for Stupidity*. I promise you'll find some exceptional ideas you can put to work immediately to improve your relationships with co-workers, spouses, employees, and family members.

–Karla Callahan, IT, American Airlines

I have had the opportunity to see Eric speak publicly and he has a phenomenal approach to explaining brain science as it relates to communication—or lack thereof. We all view the world differently, so it's only fitting that each of us processes information and communication differently.

–David Schwartz, Principal, Goodman Schwartz Public Affairs

Eric has been an astute student and teacher with a knack for weaving disparate perspectives into a cohesive whole. Couple that with his inherent good will and this book delivers a series of powerful messages.

–Randy Currier, PhD, Psychologist

The Cure for Stupidity is a fantastic, fast read. You should add it to your executive reading list immediately. If you believe culture is a big part of your success, then this book is a must read. The tools, stories, and strategies in this book will become part of your corporate language.

–Scott Grondin, Owner, Clean Freak Car Wash

Even though *The Cure for Stupidity* is intended for the workplace, the information is definitely valuable to experiences in our personal lives. As I learn about my blind spots, I am encouraged about the potential good that our tribe or community can go toward. We need relief from our divisive changes politically. This book takes a step in the right direction.

–Rose H. Bailey, DDS

The Cure for
STUPIDITY

Using Brain Science to Explain
Irrational Behavior at Work

ERIC M. BAILEY

PEACOCK PROUD
P · R · E · S · S

PHOENIX, ARIZONA

Editors:
Laura L. Bush, PhD, PeacockProud.com
Evelyn Jeffries
Wendy Ledger, VoType.com

Cover and Interior Layout:
Melinda Tipton Martin, MartinPublishingServices.com

Portrait Photographer:
Damian Serafine, serafinephotography.smugmug.com

DISCLAIMER:

To Jamie, my wife, my partner, my feedback loop, my mirror to help me see my own lack of understanding. You may never know the impact you have had on my life, but please know that without your encouragement, attention to detail, and focus on timelines, this book could not have happened. Thank you for enduring the early mornings, the late nights, the, over, use, of, commas and the seemingly endless revisions. Thank you for always being in my corner, even if it meant letting me learn a hard lesson by making a mistake (that you saw coming). Thank you for being my person. 2

Contents

Introduction

"The menace to understanding is not so much ignorance
as the illusion of knowledge."

—Daniel J. Boorstin,
Hidden History: Exploring Our Secret Past

To make sure you are qualified to read this book, let's start with an exercise in reading comprehension. The italicized paragraph below is comprised of three sentences with six punctuation marks. As you read through it, I would like you to identify the punctuation marks as you react to the message in the sentence. You can identify them by speaking them out loud as if you're doing voice dictation: "Finally [comma] Eric Bailey delivers . . . of other people [period]," etc.:

> Finally, Eric Bailey delivers us a method of understanding ourselves from the perspective of other people. First we have the fear of failure, the debilitating emotion that comes from not getting something right. But even more powerful is a force that often prevents us from stepping into our fullest potential—the fear of being successful.

Okay, here's the part where things get interesting. I would like you to read through the sentences again, ignoring punctuation, and simply count the number of f's in the paragraph:

Finally, Eric Bailey delivers us a method of understanding ourselves from the perspective of other people. First, we have the fear of failure, the debilitating emotion that comes from not getting something right. But even more powerful is a force that often prevents us from stepping into our fullest potential—the fear of being successful.

Please look at the list of options and identify which number is the correct answer:

10 11 12 13 14 15 16 17 18 19 20

The correct answer is seventeen. There are seventeen f's in the italicized paragraph. Now, I don't have the ability to watch your reaction, because that would be creepy, but I do know that most people get it wrong.

If you haven't already flipped back to check me, let me point out where those "f's" are.

Finally, Eric Bailey delivers us a method of understanding ourselves From the perspective of other people. First we have the Fear of Failure, the debilitating emotion that comes From not getting something right. But even more powerFul is a Force that oFten prevents us From stepping into our Fullest potential: The Fear of being successFul.

You're thinking, "Ummm, Eric, that's only thirteen."
Yes, I know, I'm not done yet.

Finally, Eric Bailey delivers us a method oF understanding ourselves From the perspective oF other people. First we have the Fear oF Failure, the debilitating emotion that comes From not getting something right. But even more powerFul is a Force that oFten prevents us From stepping into our Fullest potential: The Fear oF being successFul.

"What the "of's?"

Why do most of us not count the "of's"? Because whenever possible, our human brains take shortcuts. We do this because there is literally too much information in the world for our brains to comprehend. If we took in all the visual, auditory, and contextual information we encounter, our brains would explode! Not literally. Heck, most of us have a hard time staying focused all the way through a conversation with our significant other!

But as we read the phrase, the shortcuts our brain takes are "fear" (that's an f), "failure" (that's an f), "of" (that's a v). Many of our brains skip over the "f "in "of" because the shortcut is to unconsciously identify it as a "v," and it's therefore non-essential for the task at hand.

Because of the impact of phenomena like the counting of the "f's" exercise, I have developed the **Principles of Human Understanding**, a communication methodology that provides twenty-two distinct tools that you can use to understand the behaviors, decisions, and motivations of the people around you so that you can have more meaningful and effective interactions with them. Additionally, each Principle of Human Understanding, which I've classified under four main categories—**Observation Trap Principles**, **Orientation Trap Principles**, **Decision Trap Principles**, and **Action Trap Principles**—will help you understand yourself, so you can take a self-aware approach to interacting with the world around you. To help you navigate your way through the principles, I provide a list at the end of this introduction and each chapter of the book that summarizes each principle I have covered so far.

These twenty-two principles and tools are universal. They apply to all of us and are based in brain science, an interdisciplinary field that includes psychology, neuroscience, anthropology, linguistics, philosophy, and computer science. When used properly, the Principles of Human Understanding will help you improve your relationships on a practical and emotional level and can help eliminate endless frustration for you and others, both at work and at home.

The counting of the "f's" exercise is actually a wonderful demonstration of the first Principle of Human Understanding—what I call the "Illusion of Certainty," which comes from a common psychological principle first called the "Illusion of Knowledge" by researcher Daniel J. Boorstin.[1] As adults, our brains like to project certainty, even when we are uncertain. But because we also like to know things (we like to be right and to appear capable when people ask us questions), we look to provide an answer. Then when we have an answer (show that we know something), we frequently become more confident (more certain) that we are right.

Here's how the Illusion of Certainty principle can play out in the workplace: If someone owes you an assignment or project, she might tell you when she will complete it. In doing so, she sets your expectations. That's the illusion. Her brain projects certainty, and she gives you a date. In reality, she isn't sure when she will complete the project. In order to respond to you at this moment, she doesn't have the time to factor in all the steps or the potential delays, but she wants to give you an answer. When she then misses her own self-imposed deadline and loses credibility with you, that's the consequence of the Illusion of Certainty for her and for you.

Consider another example of a conversation in which someone shares a new idea or insight with the group and the first several comments about his idea are something to the effect of, "Oh, yeah. We've done that before with our team," or "We thought that exact same thing." Rather than allowing someone's shared information to wash over them as something novel for consideration, the listeners' brains project that they have already exhausted the utility of the idea and have nothing more to learn from it. That's the Illusion of Certainty at work.

The Illusion of Certainty is the first of the Principles of Human Understanding because it's important that you understand it from the start. Why? Because if you're anything like me or the people I work with, you pick up a book like this one and wonder if it's going to be worth your time. After reading the first chapter (or even just a few pages), you decide you already know what the book is going to teach you. Then as you look back through the table of contents, you might think, "I know that," "I've heard of that," "That sounds vaguely familiar," and so on. This book can change your world if, and only if, you understand this first foundational concept: the only things in life that you can learn are things that you don't yet know. Therefore, growth happens in the space of things that you don't yet know. Seek out that which you don't yet know.

The Illusion of Certainty is ever present, trying to convince us that we know everything. If that were true, there would be nothing left to learn. It's likely that you know some of what this book has to offer, and the Illusion of Certainty will highlight all that you already know. However, even if you know 80 percent of what I will discuss with you in this book, I invite you to read with an open mind and focus on the 20 percent that is new or different. That's your opportunity for growth. When you truly understand the nature and ubiquity of the Illusion of Certainty, you will recognize that there is likely much in this world that you don't yet know—and realize that you want to read on.

Principles of Human Understanding

The Observation Trap Principles

Can trap us by influencing the way we observe the world.

1. The Illusion of Certainty

CHAPTER 1

Perception

"It used to be, everyone was entitled to their own opinion,
but not their own facts. But that's not the case anymore.
Facts matter not at all. Perception is everything."

–Stephen Colbert

Perception and Reality

We've all heard the phrase "perception equals reality" or some derivative of it, right? Well, in "reality," that phrase is a lie. Perception does *not* equal reality. If you dive into the definitions of the two words "perception" and "reality," you will see that reality *excludes* perception.

Perception: A way of understanding or interpreting things.

Reality: The state of things as they actually exist, **rather than *as they may be perceived*** or *might be imagined*.

"Okay, Eric," you might say. "But my perception *is* my reality!" I'm glad you brought that up. What the phrase "My perception is my reality" actually means is this: "My perception is the genesis of my worldview. My perception is the way I believe the world to be. My perception is the basis on which I am going to interact with the world." Many people interchange the terms "truth," "fact," and "belief" because worldview is such a powerful force, which is the reason "truth" can be such a fluid concept in many contentious conversations. "If I don't believe in something, it must not be true." Or, "If I don't believe it to be true, the facts don't matter."

To illustrate, is it perception or reality that makes you freak out because of that tiny displaced hair on your neck? Or was that feeling on your neck actually a small spider crawling across your skin, its thin delicate legs almost imperceptibly touching you, sending you a sudden signal to swat at your neck? The sensation you experience is real, but it's based on a perception. There is no spider in reality, but you still adjust and protect your body based on a perception. You might even scratch an itch that materializes as you're reading. In fact, as I've been writing this, I've scratched both sides of my neck, my right shoulder, my left hip, my calf, the back of my head, and my right shoulder—again! #HeebieJeebies Okay. MOVING ON.

Perception drove me to action. I perceived an itch, even though there really wasn't anything there to cause it, and then I scratched. Perception guided my behavior, not reality.

If you don't yet believe me that perception doesn't equal reality, let me give you a visual example:

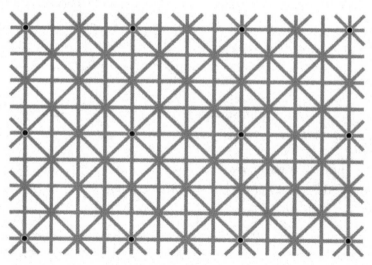

This image is a recreation of the extinction illusion created by Jaques Ninio and Kent Stevens in 2000.[2] It is commonly called "the twelve dots illusion" because if you look around the image, you notice that there are twelve black dots evenly spaced around the image. The interesting thing is that you cannot see all twelve at the same time. In fact, as you focus your vision on one, others disappear from your peripheral vision. What you perceive isn't necessarily reality. You can perceive only four to six dots at any one time, but in reality, there are twelve. This illusion leans on our poor peripheral vision and the ability of our brains to fill in missing information. Your brain sees straight gray lines and continues the lines for you through your peripheral vision, literally erasing the dots that are there in reality.

Now you can see that perception doesn't equal reality, but that's not the real lesson. The real lesson is that reality doesn't mean as much as we think it does when analyzing human behavior. When we come face-to-face with the reality that our perceptions are wrong, many of us dig in our heels and look for more evidence that our perceptions are, in fact, correct. This is an effect that psychologists have named the "biased assimilation effect."[3] When confronted with an opposing belief, we are inclined to harden our resolve that our opinion is correct. Think back to your original response to the revelation that there were 17 f's in the paragraph. "No way! That can't be. You must be mistaken." Our brains have a hard time accepting that our perceptions are wrong. This happens because our ego has a grip on us and doesn't want to let go.

Our ego's grip on us also explains why, when we have political debates with friends and family over Facebook or dinner, we have almost zero impact on their point of view, but we run the tremendous risk of destroying the good will between us. We'll dive deeper into this phenomenon in a later chapter.

How Could You Possibly?

When someone says or does something crazy or unexpected, we say, "How could you possibly think that was the right thing to say/do?" or "How could you possibly see it that way?" That phrase, "How could you possibly?" seems completely benign on the surface, but the underlying meaning comes through loud and clear. The subtext of "How could you possibly...?" is "You're an idiot." We don't often call people "stupid" to their face. We sure as heck think it though, don't we? Sometimes we think it very hard! While our mouths are saying, "How could you possibly react that way?" our brains are thinking, "You idiot."

This type of thinking happens all the time between bosses and subordinates. When a boss gives instructions to a team member, the instructions make perfect sense . . . to the boss. Because the boss can see it from her own perspective, her perception of the words she spoke perfectly convey what she was thinking in her head: "Sharon, please cut the sandwich into quarters and deliver it to Table Four." Sharon cuts the sandwich into quarters diagonally, leaving the crusts on and delivering it on a saucer to Table Four. Her manager, however, meant "Cut off the crusts, cut it into quarter squares, and deliver it on a lunch plate with fries." The problem is that Sharon perceived the words differently than her manager intended them. Sharon interpreted her perception into her actions. Far too often, the employee fails to meet the expectations of the manager because she doesn't truly understand what her manager said or wanted. Who is at fault? It doesn't really matter, because in most workplace scenarios like this, it's the manager who has the power. The manager can get frustrated at her employee for not meeting her expectations, and the employee is at her manager's mercy to figure it out. If the manager wants better outcomes, however, it's she who has the opportunity to communicate differently so that her words are perceived differently.

The point here is that it's hard for us to understand that another person perceives the world differently from us. We understand differences in perception conceptually, but when we're tested in a practical situation, things become more difficult. This happens because we spend our entire lives interacting with the world around us through our perceptions, and our perceptions guide our behaviors. The lesson here is the second Principle of Human Understanding: Perception Does Not Equal Reality; Perception Is More Important Than Reality.

Communication

Do you remember the game "Telephone" or "Operator"? That's the game in which everyone sits in a circle, and one person whispers a phrase to the next person. That person whispers it to the next person, and the message travels around the circle until the last person says it aloud. The fun part comes when the message is totally changed by the time it gets transmitted to the people toward the end of the circle. Usually, there are a few moments of blaming and finger pointing at the people who messed up the message. But in my vast "Telephone" experience, there were always two people who never messed up the message—the first person (who generated the message) and whoever claimed (incorrectly) that he didn't mess it up. It usually goes something like this: "I didn't mess it up. I passed along exactly what she said!" We've all said it, or at least thought it. But it's not true. We didn't pass along exactly what she said—we passed along exactly what we thought we heard. In other words, we don't pass along reality. We only have our perceptions at our actionable disposal.

Now, this isn't to say that your perceptions never accurately match reality, because they often do. But what you can realize here is that, as in the game "Telephone," the information that you act on is based on your perceptions, not necessarily reality. When you put this realization in the context of human communication, you can discover that what you say or do matters less than what the other person hears or feels. What you say or do is reality (with a bit of context thrown in), and what they hear is their perception. In other words, what they will act on is what they hear or feel. The implications of this knowledge are powerful. Think about any argument that you've had with a loved one. At some point, the argument usually includes, "That's not what I said!" Understanding this second principle, that Perception is More Important Than Reality, you can see that it doesn't matter what you say. It only matters what they *heard* you say because they will base their behavior on their perceptions.

> "I've learned that people will forget what you said,
> and they will forget what you did, but they will
> never forget how you made them feel."
>
> –Maya Angelou

The Fight to Be Right

Frequently, conversations or discussions devolve into arguments at a very critical moment—the moment when we feel we have been wronged. At that point, we begin to let go of our desire to solve the problem and start to focus on an entirely different goal—being right.

An argument exists because we believe we're right. The problem is that those we're arguing with also believe they are right, and we go back and forth trying to impart our rightness on the other person. Here's a skeletal representation of most arguments:

"I'm right!"

"No, I'm right!"

"No, shut up! *I'm* right."

"No, *you* shut up! *I'm* right."

"No, here's why I'm right."

"Well, here's why *I'm* right, and here's why *you're* wrong."

"Well. . . You always show up late to meetings!"

When you read that dialogue, you can almost imagine the tennis ball being smacked back and forth between the two individuals. These two people are no longer trying to solve the problem. They are not listening to each other; they have their next point ready, and they're just waiting for their turn to talk. They are competing. They're each trying to WIN. Let me ask you a question. In any sport or game, if one team is the winner, what does that make the other team? The LOSER! Rather than trying to solve the problem, they are engaged in the Third Principle of Human Understanding: The Desire to Fight to Be Right.

As leaders and managers, our fundamental duty is to bring out the best in the organization. When our employees are struggling, it's imperative that we help them thrive instead. When productivity drops, it's our responsibility to discover the problem and improve conditions, as well as relationships.

Imagine this scenario at work. Walking up to the break room, you hear the unmistakable sound of arguing. You know it's not yelling, but you're sure that it's not just talking. As you enter, you look to your left and see Karl and Samantha standing in adversarial positions. Samantha is aggressively leaning towards Karl, supporting herself with her right hand on the counter. She's standing at an almost impossible angle as she holds a crumpled piece of paper with her left hand. Karl is standing square to Samantha, with his hands making such rigid punctuated gestures that they could be meat cleavers. As you get closer, you overhear the two of them arguing over the best way to keep the coffee maker clean.

As you observe, you see the conversation devolve from the coffee maker, to overall cleanliness, to Karl's lack of intelligence, to Samantha's bossy personality. What you're witnessing is that both Karl and Samantha are fighting to be right. They are trying to be the winner and make the other person a loser. In any relationship, personal or professional, would you want to be connected with a loser? Is the organization, team, or marriage better for having a loser in it? Of course not! And yet, we still fight tooth and nail in arguments because we want to be right and win, and we certainly don't want to lose. All of us have a natural tendency to compete—that's how species survive and thrive. The winners live and pass on their genes and the losers, well . . . they lose. In our modern world, we no longer have to outrun the hungry saber-toothed tiger; we just have to outrun the next guy and not be the loser. In many situations, to avoid being the loser, we humans do whatever we can to win and make the other person lose.

Switching Tracks

Another amazing skill that we practice in the middle of arguments is the art of changing the subject. Sheila Heen, a Harvard Law School lecturer, coined the psychological concept "switchtracking" to explain this process.[4] When any conversation is headed in one direction like a train, and someone hits the "track switch" lever, all of a sudden, the conversation heads in a completely different direction. Heen explains how we often unintentionally "switchtrack" to protect ourselves from being wrong or from being attacked. Switchtracking is a common practice in conversations in which one person reacts to feedback from the other by instantly and unconsciously redirecting the topic of conversation. One person makes a critical comment to another person, and in response, the second person asks a question of the first person, which steers the conversation to another topic entirely.

Take this example:

> John is frustrated with his employee Sarah, who is late turning in her assigned project for the third time this year. "What's going on?" John asks. "Why is it that you keep turning your projects in late?"
>
> "When I schedule time to work on my projects," Sarah responds, a little defensively, "Xavier is always talking on

the phone so loudly that it disrupts the entire office. It's so frustrating that nobody ever talks to Xavier about how distracting he can be."

"You know," John responds, "Xavier has also been criticized for eating at his desk and spilling on his computer. But he's such a good employee I hate to have to reprimand him."

The worst part about conversations like this one is that often, John will engage in the conversation about Xavier, either giving his opinion or even defending Xavier. In doing so, the conversation has switched track from discussing Sarah's work habits to discussing Xavier's work habits. The benefit for Sarah is that the more the conversation stays away from her, the less likely it is for her to get in trouble. The detriment to John is that the more the conversation stays away from Sarah, the less likely it is that she will learn the time management lesson and improve her working behavior and/or her ability to communicate directly with Xavier and ask him, politely, to tone it down.

Switchtracking is something that occurs frequently in arguments, but you've also probably seen it happen in contentious political interviews on TV. According to many viewers, it can be maddening to watch a political surrogate evade questions by bringing up facts outside the original question. If you understand switchtracking, it makes perfect sense that the speakers are using these tactics. If the motive behind the question is to force someone to acknowledge or admit something negative, the protective nature of these surrogates is to avoid that negative perception. So they deploy switchtracking to make sure that the conversation stays in the realm of the positive, rather than actually playing defense against the negative. Politicians and political pundits are probably the most proficient at switchtracking, followed by spouses and children (kidding).

Switchtracking can also happen in personal conversations when one person tries to deliver critical feedback, and the reaction to the feedback is criticism about how the feedback was delivered. For instance, consider this conversation between spouses:

> Susan says, "Thanks for the bracelet, Karen, but you know I don't like rose gold. I've told you that hundreds of times."
>
> "You really should say 'thank you,'" Karen responds defensively. "I mean, it's the thought that counts, right? Do you know how long I searched to pick out that bracelet? I really thought you'd be more appreciative."
>
> "I *am* appreciative; it's just that I don't like rose gold. After all these years, you should know that by now!"
>
> "It sure doesn't sound like you're appreciative!"

Susan and Karen are on totally different tracks. The meaning behind Susan's words are that she doesn't feel that Karen listens to her, while Karen doesn't feel Susan appreciates her. Although this couple is technically in the same conversation, they are speaking and listening to each other on two totally different tracks. And as long as they stay on different tracks, the likelihood that they will achieve resolution is dreadfully low. The likelihood that they will both be fighting for RIGHT—and both actually *be* right—is very high. The best way to address switchtracking is to try to understand what the other person perceives.

What They Perceive

When you understand that when you're speaking, what you say or do matters less than what your listeners hear or feel, you begin to realize that when they hear you incorrectly, the problem doesn't lie with them. The burden to fix the problem is on you. At that point, instead of fighting, ask them questions to identify what it was about the words you said that made them feel that way. A simple apology might be a good start: "I'm sorry, I don't seem to have said that very well. What did you understand me to say?" Or perhaps, "Was it something about the words I chose that made you feel that way?"

Every one of us has a set of experiences that we call life—unique experiences that ultimately shape the way we perceive the world. This means that every one of us will perceive the world in slightly different ways. And if perception guides our behaviors, then people who perceive things differently from us will behave in ways that we do not expect. Frequently, these unexpected reactions seem to us to be irrational and cause us frustration. But now, armed with this information about perception, we can anticipate their behavior in unexpected and empowering ways.

Non-Common-Sensical

Close your eyes and imagine the sky during the daytime on a clear day. What color would you say the sky is? Most of us would say that the sky is blue. But what if it isn't? A linguist by the name of Guy Deutscher shared in his 2010 book, *Through the Language Glass*, a language experiment that he did with his daughter Alma.[5] Guy and his wife, Janie, raised Alma without ever teaching her that the sky is blue, taking intentional care not to utter the phrases that would indicate a blue sky. They taught her all the colors—blues, greens, yellows, reds, purples, and all the other colors—but never taught her explicitly the phrase "the sky is blue." One day, when Guy and Alma were on a walk, he asked, "Honey, what color is the sky?"

Alma looked at him puzzled, then looked out the window, shrugged her shoulders, and said, "I don't know. White?"

Because she had never been taught the distinction that the sky is blue, she didn't see the same blue sky that we all perceive. Distinction is how we mentally separate or distinguish one thing from another. As we learn language, our brains are making distinctions and definitions along the way. As infants, when our eyes are first developing, we begin to distinguish between this blobby-looking thing with big teeth and the lighter colored hair and that blobby-looking thing with big teeth and darker hair. Eventually, that distinction becomes "Mama" and "Dada." Throughout the rest of our lives, we begin to acquire language in the same way, using words to help us distinguish between things. The fourth Principle of Human Understanding: The Power of Distinction, is based on the idea that absent distinction, we have a difficult time making sense of the world.

You Blue It

William Gladstone, a scholar and author who would later become the British prime minister, studied Homer's *The Odyssey* and *The Iliad*. In his 1858 book, *Studies on Homer and the Homeric Age*,[6] he analyzed every word in these ancient Greek texts and found something surprising. Never once was there a mention of a color called "blue." In fact there's even a passage that says the sea was "deep wine." Deep wine? I don't know how your week has been so far, but you might be enjoying some deep wine as you read this book. One thing's for sure, though, wine is not blue! Most of us would say that the seas, oceans, and sky, however, *are* blue. According to Gladstone, in all of Homer's color references, there were over two hundred mentions of black or dark, over one hundred mentions of white or light. There were even mentions of reds, yellows, and greens. And yet nowhere in Homer's *The Odyssey* or *The Iliad* is a single mention of the color blue. Curious.

Two years after Gladstone's book, a German philologist named Lazarus Geiger continued the research by looking at other ancient texts. Philology is the study of language through literary history. He reviewed Icelandic sagas, the ancient Hebrew Bible, ancient Chinese texts, and ancient Hindu Vedic hymns. Never once in any of those ancient writings was there mention of the color blue. The word just didn't exist. Again, curious.

Some folks often draw the conclusion that ancient humans couldn't see blue, but that was not the case. In fact, in the developmental history of every single language, the last color word defined is "blue." The impact of this phenomenon is greater than researchers originally thought. For insight into this, we look to Dr. Jules Davidoff's 2005 experiments on *Color Categories: Evidence for the Cultural Relativity Hypothesis* and travel to Namibia to meet the Himba people.[7]

The Himba tribe is a modern nomadic tribe on the western coast of Africa. They are genetically modern Homo sapiens. Dr. Jules Davidoff visited them and learned their language in the same way that we would learn any language, mapping English words to Himba words. When he got to identifying colors, things got interesting. He showed them three color swatches with various shades of green, and they mapped out the words buru, dambu, and zuzu. When he showed them the color swatch for blue, they looked at him with a look that said, "You already showed us that color," and added, "That's buru." While this language has three different color words for various shades of green, they do not have a unique word for the color blue. Even more curious.

So Dr. Davidoff went a little further and sat them down in front of a computer (which I can only imagine freaked them out a little). Then he gave them a color recognition test. First, he showed them a ring of green color swatches with one blue swatch and asked them to identify which square was different from the others. They laughed at him, as if to say, "You've made a mistake! They're all the same, you silly American!" But of course, they're not all the same! Because they did not have the language to distinguish blue from green, they literally could not see the difference between the two colors. In other words, without distinction, humans don't even know what we're missing. We are effectively blind to what other people can see clearly.

This Is Garbage

I want to tell you a personal story about distinction. One of my jobs around the house is to collect the trash on Thursdays. To do my job, I go around the house and collect all the little trash cans. Then I transfer the garbage from those trash cans into one trash bag that I take out to the dumpster before pulling the dumpster out to the curb. Well, one Thursday afternoon my wife Jamie says, "Eric, I have a pet peeve I want to talk with you about." Now, "pet peeve" is the terminology Jamie and I use to indicate that we are frustrated, but we're intentionally not becoming mad. I kind of knew what was coming, so I took a breath and prepared myself, "Yes. . . ?"

"Eric," she explained, "you never put away the downstairs bathroom trash when you're done with it."

"Yeah," I admitted. "I guess, if I'm in a hurry, I'm going from one trash can to the other. I maybe forget it, but I'll definitely work on it!"

The next Thursday came around, and I put the downstairs bathroom trash can right there between the sink and the toilet. Boom! I puffed up my chest because I knew that I was a good husband. I felt proud of myself. Later that afternoon, though, Jamie came up to me and said, "Eric, I thought we talked about this. You didn't put the trash can away again!"

Now, I completely wheeled around and said, "That can't be true! I know I did."

"Come on, let's go look."

"Yeah," I said with a twinge of defiance. "Let's go look." (Fight for Right.)

We walked into the downstairs bathroom and she pointed at the trash can without saying a word.

"See?" I triumphantly exclaimed. "It's right there."

Then, almost rolling her eyes, Jamie pointed to the trash can and echoed, "See?"

At that point, I realized I was missing something and must have had a confused look on my face. Then she did something amazing; she gave me a distinction: "Do you realize that when I bought this trash can, I found one that was twelve inches wide and six inches deep, perfectly sized to fit between the toilet and the sink like this?" She then repositioned the trash can between the toilet and the sink, so the twelve-inch width filled the entire space. She continued, "You keep putting the trash can away like this." My wife then rotated the rectangular trash can the way I had positioned it so now the twelve-inch width was sticking out pretty far into the bathroom. "When you put the trash can that way," she explained, "the kids kick it and knock it over, spilling the contents all over the floor. I'm usually the one that has to pick the trash up."

"Ohhhhhhhhhhhh!" I suddenly realized. Her point hit me. I once was blind, but now I see! There *was* a right way to position the trash can, but I never even realized there could be a wrong way. I was so focused on putting the can in the right space that I never even realized that orientation mattered. When you zoom out a bit on this situation, you see that to Jamie, I was making a common-sense error, but I didn't even know that there was an error that could be made. Without such a distinction, I couldn't know what I was missing.

The lesson is this: when you give someone a direction, and they miss some stupid, common-sense detail (to *you*), chances are they missed that detail because they didn't have the same distinction that you do. Instead of saying, "How could you possibly. . . ?" realize that without distinction, they're effectively blind, but it's not their fault. To Jamie, I was making a common-sense error. But it only seemed that way to her because she had a distinction that I didn't have. Her perception was different from mine.

The same thing happens in workplaces every single day. Remember Karl and Samantha in the break room? Well, I shared that the two were arguing over how to clean the coffee maker, but I never explained how their conversation became an argument. Hint: common sense.

Karl is known around the office as a neat freak. Coworkers often use the word "retentive" to describe him. When Karl walked into the break room in the morning, he saw that the coffee pot was not emptied and rinsed at the end of the day. On top of that, the pot was now stained with a thin brown ring of nastiness. Since this was the tenth time that this nastiness had happened in the past month, Karl decided to write a note and tape it to the coffee maker to declare his frustration: "Please don't be an animal! Clean and rinse the coffee maker after 4:00 p.m." In Karl's mind, it's common sense that if the coffee maker doesn't get cleaned at the end of the day, the person in the morning (him) has to spend more effort scrubbing it before he can make any coffee. "How could you possibly not know this?" thought Karl. And he was thinking that exact same thing as he was scrubbing the pot yet again. When people make common-sense errors, our natural reaction is to say, "How could you possibly not know that?" or "How could you possibly make that mistake?" Remember, the subtext of these questions is actually, "How could you be so stupid?"

When we see people we care about or people that we work with making common-sense errors, it's important to consider that it may not be the person's fault. We call it a "common-sense error" because we have some distinction that they don't yet have. Remember, though, that "The only things in life that we can learn are things that we don't yet know." You've just discovered something that they can learn. And when you understand the impact of that, then rather than assuming they are stupid, it is incumbent upon you to help them understand the distinction. What Karl and Samantha both failed to do was to explain what they saw that the other person clearly didn't see.

Karl knows that cleaning the coffee pot at the end of the day takes only a few seconds, but if the coffee sits overnight, it takes several minutes to scrub it clean. The person in the morning (usually Karl) is already making coffee for himself and everyone that comes after, so it would be nice if he didn't have to do extra, unnecessary work. Samantha, however, sees that if the coffee pot got washed out at 4:00 p.m., as Karl's sign suggested, she would just have to make more coffee because she usually drinks her last cup of coffee at 6:00 p.m. Both of them have a distinction that the other lacks. Rather than taking responsibility, Karl blamed Samantha for lacking common sense, and Samantha blamed Karl for lacking common sense.

Just like Karl and Samantha, we often become frustrated and annoyed with people who make common-sense errors. Once we understand the Power of Distinction, we can see that there is another way to react.

Principles of Human Understanding

The Observation Trap Principles

Can trap us by influencing the way we observe the world.

1. The Illusion of Certainty
2. Perception is More Important Than Reality
3. The Desire to Fight to Be Right
4. The Power of Distinction

CHAPTER 2

The Power of Meaning and Context

"All my books deal with the effect of intent upon action, how our understanding of good and evil depends heavily on context."

–Jesse Kellerman

We usually look to identify as much information as possible before making a judgment or decision, but often, we fail to seek and understand meaning. Information is a broader term that includes all facts about something or someone. Meaning, on the other hand, has more to do with underlying reasoning and context behind the information.

Crucial Conversations: Tools for Talking When Stakes Are High has been one of the most influential books on my thinking about communication at work and human relationships.[8] In this book, a group of researchers—Al Switzler, Joseph Grenny, Kerry Patterson, and Ron McMillan—introduce a concept they call the "Shared Pool of Meaning."[9] In the context of their work, they define "meaning" differently from the typical, "What do you mean?" or "What idea are you trying to express?" For them, "meaning" is more akin to "What is the underlying purpose or context of this particular communication?" They explain that each of us has our own opinions, feelings, theories, and experiences about a topic, and those opinions, feelings, theories, and experiences make up our personal "meaning." When people start having conversations (especially those that are "crucial" or important), they will be more successful if they take the opportunity to share their "meaning(s)" with each other prior to making decisions. In their research, the authors have found that the more meaning that members share among a group, the better the decisions the group will make.

To illustrate, let's say that you and I have been tasked to drive from one end of the city to another to pick up a client from the airport. As we're buckling up, you say, "Hey Eric, how do you want to get to the airport?"

I pull onto the main road and say, "I'm just going to take 7th Street." Then I drive down the road.

You think to yourself, "That's ridiculous. We'll get there way faster on the freeway. I was just asking if you wanted to take I-10 or 99."

My choice to take a surface street frustrated you because every single time that you've made that same drive, you took the freeway, which was significantly faster than surface streets. At that point, we might end up in an argument, or you might hold your tongue, silently calling me stupid the entire way.

If you and I were only to consider the objective information, we would find that it takes X number of minutes, Y number of miles, etc. to get to the airport. The miles and minutes are the information (data) that we can use to determine whether it's best to take surface streets or the freeway. Usually, each of us presents such information to justify our own reasoning for making a decision. Then the person we're arguing with gives a different set of data to prove we made the wrong decision. But, according to the authors of *Crucial Conversations*, if people deal in meaning, rather than data, they can have a different kind of conversation.

Here's an example of meaning behind my decision to take surface streets: One evening, a couple of months ago, I was driving home from the airport on a freeway marked at a relatively low speed limit for Arizona (55 mph). I was traveling in the middle lane going exactly 62 mph with my cruise control on. All of a sudden, a car approaching me from behind in the carpool lane, going about 80 mph, drifted out of its lane, across the left lane, and slammed into the back of my car. I heard a loud crunch-smack-pop sound that scared me to death. Luckily, I didn't lose control of my car. I was able to get my wits about me fast enough to pull off to the side of the road. Ultimately, the seventeen-year-old driver admitted that he was looking down at his phone at the time of the accident.

Ever since then, I've been terrified of driving on that freeway because I see how many people are looking down at their phones while they drive. So, when I need to go from point A to point B, and it's possible to take surface streets, I prefer not to take that freeway. Now, I understand that people still look down at their phones on surface streets, too, but they are not doing so while traveling at 80 mph. All of that meaning for me exists behind the decision that I usually make to not take that freeway.

Often, we only push for an idea with another person (don't take that freeway) without sharing the meaning behind why we chose that idea (I was recently in a bad accident on that freeway). When you understand the meaning behind my decision, it makes a lot more sense, doesn't it? Full disclosure: While the story of my accident is true, I'm not actually terrified to drive on the freeway. However, I have worked with several people who avoid certain roads because of previous accidents. When we take the time to understand the meaning behind their ideas, aversions, opinions, and decisions, communication is much more effective.

Similarly, it's much easier for me to understand you if you share the meaning behind your idea to take the freeway: "Google Maps says that our client's plane is going to land fifteen minutes ahead of schedule and it's possible that we're going to be late. We need to get there as quickly as possible so that we don't make a poor first impression on our new client." Now that the meaning for both people has been shared, the decision-making process is much easier, better informed, and understood. In this situation, we would take the freeway, even though it wasn't my idea. But because you considered my meaning, *and* I understood your meaning, I can get on board with the decision to take the freeway.

Meaning underlies all the decisions that people make, but we rarely take the time to share or discuss it. And often if we are making a shared decision, we don't take the time to allow everyone to share their own meaning. When group decisions are made and people don't have the opportunity to share their meaning, they are less invested in the success of the decision. Most change initiatives fail in part because employees don't understand the meaning behind the ultimate decision and were never given an opportunity to share their own ideas and meaning.

Nature AND Nurture

If there's one debate that's been raging in the scientific community, it's the conversation about Nature versus Nurture—the question of whether humans are products of their environment or products of their genetic makeup. The wonderfully simple answer to this debate, just like many others in our ambiguous adult world, is that both nature AND nurture play a part. While we are largely predestined for hair and eye color or forearm length (nature), much of our personality and behavior is governed by our experiences and surroundings (nurture). To understand how powerful nurture can be, let's think about little Johnny who is ten years old and in fifth grade. He stands about four feet, six inches tall and has dark brown curly hair, just like his mother (nature). And just like his father, Johnny has perfect vision (nature).

Johnny has always gotten decent grades in school, and after a decade of watching his mother read for at least thirty minutes each night, he, too, enjoys reading (nurture). In due course, Johnny becomes acquainted with Zachary on the first day of the second week of school. All the parents have heard stories about how Zachary is a troublemaker who must regularly visit the principal's office and, according to the kids, is also the class clown who doesn't get very good grades. After a few weeks, Johnny and Zachary become close friends. They spend every recess together and eat lunch together. Perhaps you've noticed that when we have people in our lives who are influential or admired in certain ways, we often actually start to mirror some of their behaviors. So what do you think happens to Johnny's behavior at school? He starts getting into trouble and ends up in the principal's office just like Zachary. He stops reading for pleasure. He even starts laughing like Zachary (nurture).

In contrast, if Johnny, instead, became best friends with Genevieve, who is the top reader in the school, has always gotten perfect grades, and volunteers her recess time with preschoolers, what do you think would become of Johnny? Of course, after a few weeks, Johnny would start to read more, earn better grades, and maybe consider volunteering (nurture). Obviously, this example is hypothetical, but the underlying principle is the same. When you surround yourself with people you admire (no matter the reason), you start to emulate their behavior.

In high school, for example, most of us have a memory of that one person who had a uniquely cool way of talking, or a funny laugh, or invented a silly greeting. Then that behavior started to influence the entire school over time. For me, it was my good friend from high school named Adam. He decided to make nicknames for people by chopping their last name at some random place (for me it was BAIL) and then adding a "Z." So my name was BAILZ. My friends were WALLZ, HARMZ, WILLZ, etc. It's silly, but after a while, the funny name-chopping took over, and the entire school was doing it. Honestly, as I read these nicknames back, I actually hear them in Adam's voice.

Let's apply the concept of nurture or social context in another way. Nearly all Americans (about 80 percent according to a 2017 study by Harris Poll) live paycheck to paycheck.[10] This means that right before their paycheck arrives, their bank account balance is relatively low, virtually empty. Nearly all Americans (about 80 percent, according to a Lexington Law Survey) report that they would not feel comfortable talking about money with a friend. In his book, *How Rich People Think*, Steve Siebold explains that most people feel uncomfortable talking about money with their friends because they view money as a constant burden (nurture). Wealthy people, on the other hand, view money as a tool.[11] Wealthy people teach their children how to understand and use that tool, while surrounding themselves with people who make more than they do (nurture).

Do you intentionally surround yourself with people who make more money than you? Statistically speaking, only about two out of ten people will say "yes." Most can't even answer this question because we don't talk about money with our friends, we don't know how much our friends are making (although we probably try to guess). Therefore, we do not intentionally surround ourselves with wealthy people or people who are good with their money. For the majority of us, our social context is that money is taboo, and therefore, we won't talk about it, and ultimately, we can't find freedom from its constraints.

The wealthy, however, live in a different context. Their social context (nurture) is that money is not a burden, but rather a tool that's available to use. And the people around them know how to make money, save money, and invest it. In part, because of this learned understanding, wealthy people find it easier to gain greater wealth. If you change your context, you change your outcomes.

Children are Insignificant

Have you ever stopped to think about how insignificant children are in the world? Physically, they are diminutive. Emotionally, they are immature. And mentally, they do not have the knowledge or wisdom to make a meaningful impact on society. Most importantly, as adults, we reinforce their insignificance on a daily basis.

In his 2000 research article, "Narcissism as a Motivational Structure," Dr. Jon Shaw identifies why children seem so selfish. When humans feel a sense of insignificance in the world, they create a new narrative about their lives, giving themselves more significance. Essentially, if everywhere you go, people avoid talking to you in favor of talking to your taller, more mature family members, you may start to believe that you're not important and simply disengage. If everywhere you look, you find a world that is not built for you, where the most frequent word that you hear is "NO," you will start to form a perception of the world as a place where you have to fight or act out to get attention. Unfortunately, this context is constantly reinforced. "Why do I have to say 'Dad' seven times, before he answers me? Why do I ask him to watch me do a trick, but as soon as I do it, he looks at his phone?" Many children believe that they are insignificant, and the world reinforces that belief. Why is it that we reinforce that notion, unless we also believe that it's true?

Randy, a mentor of mine, told me that his grandson loved spending time with him. After the third or fourth time I heard this statement, I finally asked Randy, "Why do you think your grandson loves spending time with you?" In jest, I said, "Is it because you always let him watch TV, or because you give him candy and money?" His answer surprised me and changed the way that I parent my children.

"No," he said. "My grandson loves spending time with me because when he talks, I give him my FULL, undivided attention. I put my phone down, make eye contact, and listen. I think that kids don't receive that very much, so he loves it." In that context, his grandson is significant, not insignificant, when he's hanging out with "Pa."

I was impressed with Randy's attention to his grandson because mostly, we adults have normalized our lives with busy on top of busy. We begin to fill every single possible gap with "stuff to do," or the thought that "I deserve a break because I'm so busy." We avoid being bored or idle, and we have a wonderful piece of technology in our hands that can almost instantly give us access to the world's news, information, and entertainment. When we are engrossed in the ghostly glow of this magical technology and the insignificant people around us call out for our attention, it takes us a few moments to divert our attention to them, if we give our attention at all. Some people around us feel insignificant, and we are continually helping them confirm they're right.

If our jobs are to raise children and grandchildren to become well-adjusted adults, why do we spend so much time reinforcing the notion that children are insignificant? When given the opportunity to choose between our children and our phones, why do we frequently choose our phones first? Why do we occasionally listen to stories or play games with only half of our attention? Think about what these decisions are doing to humans' feeling of significance.

If our view of the world is shaded by the context of insignificance, then we humans tend to lean a little harder towards achieving significance. You've probably heard of the Napoleon Complex, whereby people, usually men, who are below average height tend to be slightly more aggressive than their taller counterparts. Several research studies, including Jill Knapen, Nancy Blaker, and Mark Vugt's 2018 study, "The Napoleon Complex: When Shorter Men Take More"[12] explain this complex. However, the term "Napoleon Complex" is wrong. Napoleon did not attempt to conquer Europe because he was very short. In fact, at 5' 6.5" he was considered average height for his time. The misunderstanding about Napoleon's real height comes first, from his habit of surrounding himself with tall soldiers as guards. By comparison, he would appear shorter. Second, when measured in French units of the time, his height was 5' 2" or so. When converted, those units equal about 169 cm or 5' 6.5" in current units of measure, just slightly above the average male height in the late 1700s (5' 5.8"). While the name "Napoleon Complex" is, therefore, a misnomer, the underlying psychology remains. It harkens to a need for balance. When people feel that they are insignificant in a certain way, they are understandably compelled to create significance about their insignificance.

Remember Karl and Samantha? They both feel insignificant in their own ways. Karl believes that nobody respects or appreciates him for getting to the office early and starting the coffee every day. He believes that he's doing a great service to those that come into the office after him. His feeling of insignificance is reinforced by the extra work that is thoughtlessly dumped on him when people don't clean out the coffee pot. But with a word processor and a printer, he tries to reclaim his significance by taping a note on a coffee pot.

Like Karl, Samantha feels that nobody understands her because the late shift is always being left out and ignored. She sees Karl's note as further proof that she's thought of as insignificant. "Clean out the coffee pot at 4:00? What about those of us who work well after 4:00?" If your feeling at work is that you are insignificant, either because you have an apparently meaningless job, your boss doesn't listen to your ideas, you're constantly criticized, or you're constantly ignored, you will likely begin playing one of two roles: (1) Dominating Intelligence, "The Know-It-All" or (2) Openly Apathetic, "The Professionally Disengaged."

Dominating Intelligence, "The Know-It-All"

We have all known or been the know-it-all at some point in our lives. For instance, as soon as you read the words "know-it-all," someone probably jumped to the front of your mind. The know-it-all takes every story, hijacks it, and tells his own possibly bigger or better story. He's the one who says, "I know" to every fact that is shared (even if he doesn't know. See the "Illusion of Certainty"). The know-it-alls don't want to be surprised or impressed by your information; they do not want to give you the satisfaction of sharing something novel. They want to be the one who shares the novel information.

Here's the thing. The know-it-all is operating from a deeply rooted sense of insignificance. I'm not going to pretend that I know the deep psychological needs of every person who plays this role, but I do know that the desire to always be right often comes from a fear of being wrong. The compulsion to prove that they are smart comes from a worry that they will be seen as dumb. The need to have the best story or experience to share comes from a fear that they aren't important. It's helpful to understand that those who have a fear of being wrong rarely admit that they are wrong.

Many of us have worked on teams on which the boss, who happens to be a know-it-all, made a hiring decision that the rest of the team thought was a bad idea. If the person who made the decision felt insignificant, she might never want to admit that she was wrong. I have seen this behavior play out in a number of the jobs that I have held. Everyone could see that the new hire was failing for months, but nothing got done about it. Often, the focus of attention was directed toward the hired person because we wanted and needed improved performance, but we should also have been looking at the person who refused to admit their mistake in hiring an unqualified person in the first place.

Once I attempted to talk to our know-it-all boss about his hiring mistake and how to avoid a similar mistake in the future (as well as how to remedy the poor employee performance in the present), his response was as swift as it was defensive. He shut down the conversation almost immediately while simultaneously criticizing some of my unrelated work (switchtracking). My attempts to improve the situation had made him feel defensive and insignif-icant. He was fighting to prove otherwise. I remember telling others about how irrational his response was, and honestly, I lost a little respect for him. Ironically, because of this situation, he lost significance with me and others around the office.

Openly Apathetic, "The Professionally Disengaged"

In 1996, the Gallup Organization released Q^{12}, a twelve-question employee engagement survey that has since been used over 25 million times. Like many other engagement surveys, the results of this survey identify employees as ei-ther engaged or disengaged, but it also introduced a concept called "actively disengaged." According to Gallup's research, actively disengaged employees are more likely to steal from the company, miss more days of work, and have more accidents on the job. Since the launch of Q^{12}, there have been thousands of articles written about disengagement and active disengagement, and it has reached a point where disengagement has been called an "epidemic."

A simple Google search for "epidemic of disengagement" will lead you to hundreds of standard web results and thousands of scholarly articles. This expanding body of information leads us to believe that there is a serious and growing problem with employee engagement. However, I recently read a research article by a former professor of mine, Dr. Matthew Grawich of Saint Louis University, in which he indicated that contrary to the popular belief, the workforce is NOT becoming more disengaged.[13] That's right. NOT MORE DISENGAGED. The disengagement numbers are real, and there is a problem with disengagement, but according to Dr. Grawich's June 2017 APA Center for Organizational Effectiveness article, the idea that we, as a society, are losing our grip on employee engagement just isn't true.

There certainly are, however, people in our ranks who *are* disengaged. They show up to work as late as they can without getting in trouble, and they occupy as much of their time as possible trying to visit every single web page ever created. They Facebook, they Tweet, they play games on their phone. They do everything that they can to appear as though they're working. These are the people who have mastered the Alt+Tab keyboard shortcut to quickly switch back to the previously open application (in case anyone walks up behind them). In some organizations, these folks are actually rewarded. They are often ignored and/or avoided, which is exactly what they want. They want to fade into nothingness and have the freedom to do whatever they want without negative consequences. Their bosses intentionally ignore them, not wanting (or knowing how) to deal with the problem.

Often the disengaged "problem employee" is behaving this way because she feels ignored and insignificant. Maybe she has spent extra time putting together a report or a project that she was proud of, only to see that none of the fifty people she shared it with actually read it. Or possibly she filled out an "Employee Engagement Survey" and poured her heart into the comments about what could be done to improve morale, offering detailed accounts of issues and possible solutions. But nothing came of her efforts. Nobody mentioned the survey to her again, until the following year when managers elicited feedback—again.

I recently interviewed a group of IT professionals, and I heard story after story about how they inserted song lyrics, random names, trivia questions, and other nonsensical information into the middle of weekly reports. They said that they did this JUST to see if their managers actually read the reports. They didn't. Every anecdote had the same conclusion, not a single person noticed. What was the impact of this? They stopped putting energy into producing the reports.

These employees aren't lazy—they just feel insignificant. Remember, what you DO as a leader matters less than what your employees FEEL about it. If someone feels insignificant at work, she may come to the rational conclusion that giving any energy above the bare minimum is not worth the effort.

Learn the Language Already

How many of us as adults have attempted to learn a new language? How many of us have failed? It's probably nearly the same number. But kids learn new languages easily. Why? There is a fundamental difference between the way that children and adult brains function, and it's the reason that most adults fail the following perception test, and most children pass it.

Looking at this image, which direction is the bus traveling?

The reason children are able to answer this question at a rate of about 80 percent is due to an often ignored distinction about intelligence: "crystallized" and "fluid" intelligence.[14] Researchers John Horne and Raymond Cattell, professor and student, posit that "crystallized intelligence" is the information and understanding that comes from years of knowledge and reinforced through experience. Crystallized intelligence can help a person to solve complex problems even while missing information because his experience will help fill in any gaps. (To test your crystallized intelligence, check out the Light Switch Quiz at www.EricMBailey.com/brain). If information were like water, then information that had been used over and over again would start to turn into a solid by forming crystals. Eventually, that information becomes fully "reliable" and becomes a solid, like ice. Reliability in this case is not necessarily accurate.

As adults try to solve the bus test, the answer is unclear because we believe that there isn't enough information that we can cross reference to our bank of crystallized intelligence. So we look harder to gather more information to add to our knowledge. At this point, most adults figure that it must be a trick, and there is some obscure visual information that we are not seeing, so we look harder and scrutinize every single detail. Adults look for mirrors and traffic lane lines, we look at the bumpers and scrutinize the windows. Throughout this entire process, adults are taking in more and more information and analyzing it for clues. More often than not, adults get overwhelmed by the sheer volume of information they are trying to process and become stalled. Did you fall into what is colloquially called "Analysis Paralysis?"

Distinct from crystalized intelligence, fluid intelligence is the type of intelligence that allows us to take in new information, process it rapidly, and act on it. It is called "fluid" because it flows like liquid water, not particularly concerned about where it has been or where it ends up. Fluid intelligence is often called "street smarts." It's what we use when we are navigating a new job or a new city—we take in the new world around us and do our best to make sense of it. If we used crystallized intelligence to navigate a new job or a new city, we would try to relate what we are seeing to what we are used to seeing in our former job or home city. That's why some of us get lost in new office spaces and new cities. We expect certain things to be in certain places—the way we're used to seeing them. I'm certain that you've experienced this at one point or another in your career. An employee who joined your organization just over a year ago at every opportunity brings up examples of how things were done at his previous job. It can be incredibly frustrating. On the several times that this has happened to me, I found myself commiserating with other employees, "Geeze, if he liked it so much, why did he leave!?" I was frustrated by the apparent irrational behavior.

The reason that the bus test is so easy for children and difficult for adults is that in the first years of our lives, all we have is fluid intelligence. The world itself is new, so our worldview is fluid as we learn how to interact with it. Children look at this image and respond to the first visual clue that they see (or expect to see but don't) and draw their correct conclusion: "It's going that way."

Children know the answer because there isn't a door facing them. If they can't see the door, the door must be on the other side which means that it's going "that way." With a tiny little finger pointed to the left (or to the right in a few countries).

Side Note: If the bus is in the United States, France, or any other country where drivers drive on the right side of the road, the bus is going to the left. If the bus is in Japan, the United Kingdom, or any other country where drivers drive on the left side of the road, the bus is going to the right.

In contrast to fluid intelligence, as we gain meaningful experiences, we establish more and more crystallized intelligence. At about fourteen years of age, our balance of fluid intelligence and crystallized intelligence evens out. As we mature, we trust in our experience more and develop crystallized intelligence more rapidly than we do fluid intelligence. As children, our brains are full of fluid intelligence, making adapting to new environments and learning new languages easy. If you've ever spent time with an infant, you can see the "everything in this world is new and exciting" looks on their faces. Because everything is new, their brains are primed to take in as much as possible. They are ready to learn. Interestingly, at this age, they are adept at learning languages. Adults find learning languages is significantly harder.

For example, you've just been told you're going to be reassigned to work in your corporation's office in Japan. You're excited about the opportunity, but they've only given you six months to start learning Japanese before you go. What do you do? It's the twenty-first century, so you'll likely try using an app on your phone or a program on your computer. You might also hire tutors or attend a course at a community college. After six months of "studying," how much Japanese do you think you'll know? If you're like most folks, you'll know little more than a few survival phrases and some food words.

Learning a language as an adult is difficult because of our crystallized intelligence, but that doesn't fully explain why we often fail. We also often have difficulty in trying to learn Japanese because our context is English. As soon as we put the app down or walk out of the tutoring session, we are in an English-speaking environment, surrounded by English speakers, and English signs. The Japanese learning ends as soon as we are done with the lesson.

But what happens when you switch your brain to an environment that requires more fluid intelligence and change your context? What happens if you actually go to work in Japan? Every time you leave your apartment, everyone around you is speaking Japanese. (Yes, I know many people in Japan speak English, too, but a vast majority of the ambient language you'd hear will be Japanese.) After about a week or two, you'd be able to survive. The best part about immersing yourself in a new context is what happens after a few months: you will actually start to dream in Japanese. It's a bizarre phenomenon, because our native language is so ubiquitous that most of us don't even think about the language in our dreams. Then when our dream language changes, it's revolutionary! After about a year or two, you'll be fluent and will likely know the language for the rest of your life. That is the power of context. When, as adults, our context is Japanese, we learn Japanese. When our context is English, it's incredibly difficult to learn Japanese. So take that transfer to Japan and start learning Japanese.

Now, context isn't only about learning languages. Context is the underlying fabric by which we encounter the world. This is my fifth Principle of Human Understanding. Context can be a mindset established by experience or the feelings that shape someone's body language. Context can be the culture of your organization or the roles and routines in your relationships.

People ask me all the time, "How can we develop a culture of innovation in my organization?" The first thing I do is evaluate the context (or the current culture). I ask people how comfortable they feel sharing ideas. I ask employees if they feel free to voice an opinion contrary to the opinion their boss espouses. I ask them what "accountability" means. What I find is that employees in most organizations are unwilling to try new ideas and be accountable for them because they are worried about how it will look if they fail. When employees are unwilling to share their innovative ideas, it's usually because they've had their ideas shot down (or they've seen other ideas shot down), and they are afraid of embarrassment.

People want a culture of innovation, but sometimes the context of their organization is fear and/or a lack of trust. When employees are concerned that one mistake may cost them their job (or embarrassment), the likelihood that they will boldly propose innovative ideas is next to zero. When the word "accountability" becomes synonymous with "blame," people will be especially wary of taking risks. If you want to change your culture, pay attention to the context. Context is not just a major part of culture; it plays a big role in our conversations as well.

As the underlying fabric, context can take many forms. One of them is nonverbal or body language. When people talk, the words are the content, but the underlying non-verbal communication and the listener's past experiences make up the context. As listeners, we are constantly evaluating the situation for content and context. "Did they roll their eyes?" "I wonder why they said it that way." "This sounds just like last time when she said . . . ." When we are communicating, it's important that we realize that our content is not the only thing that our listeners are paying attention to. Does our tone sound calm, frustrated, angry, accusatory, or something else? Is our body position aggressive? Are our words authentic or are we dancing around the subject? Remember that the definition of perception is "a way of understanding or interpreting things." As people listen to us, they are interpreting both the content and the context. They are hearing the words that we are using as well as the tone with which we are saying them. Additionally, our words are passing through the filter of their past experiences.

We're back in the break room, and Samantha has just walked in after starting her shift at 9:00 a.m. She sees a posted sign on the coffee maker that reads, "Don't be an Animal! Clean the Coffee Pot after 4:00 p.m." Samantha is livid. She's one of several employees that work four ten-hour shifts starting at 9:00 a.m. She's typically still at work at 8:00 p.m. "How could someone possibly think that cleaning the coffee pot at 4:00 p.m. is remotely a good thing? Once again," she thinks to herself in a huff, "the people with the better schedules don't even consider us!" Furious, Samantha tears off the sign and walks over to throw it in the recycle bin just as Karl enters the break room for another cup of coffee.

Sometimes when people react to something that we said in ways that we deem "irrational," it may be because they are reacting to some contextual clues that we didn't intend to deliver. Similarly, when we overreact to something, it is because we are picking up on contextual cues. In the case of Samantha and Karl, a lot of uncommunicated context is present between them. First, Samantha believes from her past experience, that late-shift folks are being ignored and left out of consideration. Second, Karl believes he is doing a service to the entire office by being the first person in every morning and making the first pot of coffee. Third, the use of the word "animal" triggers a lot of emotion based on past experience for Samantha. Fourth, Karl believes that the coffee pot is being left at the end of the day because people assume that he will clean it. All this meaning triggers both Karl and Samantha to react in irrational (i.e. stupid) ways to a seemingly "small" problem like a dirty coffee pot.

The Perception Escalator™

Step 1: Action—First some action occurs in the world. Something happens.

Step 2: Perception—We perceive that action through our senses, our contextual filters, and our experiences.

Step 3: Story—We tell a story about our perception, making sense of our perception.

Step 4: Judgment—We make some judgment about the story. Like good or bad, right or wrong.

Step 5: Feeling—Based on our judgment, we experience a feeling about the situation. Feeling like happy, sad, annoyed, frustrated, elated, insecure, etc.

Step 6: Reaction—Once we experience a feeling, we believe we fully understand the situation, and we react.

I call this the "Perception Escalator," and you know that escalators are essentially treadmill stairs, so the steps go up and around and down, up and around and down, up and around and down, and so on. Based on our reaction, which happens in an instant, the process starts again. Someone else perceives our reaction. Based on her perception, she tells a story, makes a judgment, experiences a feeling, and in turn, has her own reaction.

There are many places along this process where things can go awry. But it's important to know that actions and reactions are the only things that can actually be measured in the real world. Perceptions, judgments, and stories are interpretations of reality, and feelings are emotions that get attached to stories. All the steps between action and reaction happen within our own brains. Of all six steps, stories are what cause the most irrational (and seemingly stupid) behavior because the stories that we tell about a situation affect how we feel and ultimately how we react.

PAUL'S STORY

Friday morning, Paul jumped into his Camry to head into work. It was one of those beautiful mid-spring mornings when the songbirds are weaving a chorus of delightful chirps and whistles, celebrating the sixth mid-70-degree day in a row. As Paul backed out of his driveway, a wave of delight washed over him as he remembered because he left the house on time, he could take the scenic route to work through the orange orchard and because the weather was so nice he could drive with the windows down and enjoy the fragrant aroma of citrus blossoms on the way to work.

Paul turned onto Orchard Drive with his left elbow proudly protruding over the window of his car and for a split second, he closed his eyes as he inhaled the lovely smells of spring. After a few seconds of accelerating on this utopian drive, his car was up to 40 miles per hour, and he engaged his cruise control. At that exact moment, a large black diesel truck roared up in his rear-view mirror, apparently trying to drive over him as if it were a monster truck rally. At the last moment, as another car was coming in the opposite direction, a plume of black smoke billowed out of the truck's left-facing exhaust pipe, and the truck swerved to the right and accelerated on the shoulder past Paul's Camry, spewing diesel smoke into Paul's open windows. Seemingly in an instant, the truck was a mile up the road.

Paul's wonderful mood evaporated. "Are you KIDDING ME? What's wrong with that guy? He's a maniac with obvious anger issues! And he nearly ran me into oncoming traffic!"

For the remainder of the drive, Paul replayed the scenario over and over, fuming about the danger that idiot put him in. But as soon as the anger subsided a little, he caught a whiff of the acidic smell of the diesel exhaust trapped in his car, and the emotion came flooding back.

When Paul finally arrived at work, he had a searing headache. He wasn't sure if it was from five minutes of unreleased anger or from the fumes that he could still smell on his clothes. Either way, it made him even madder at the man in the black truck, whom he now hated. Not wanting to engage with anyone, Paul went directly to his office, muttering a terse "hello" to everyone who had the nerve to speak to him.

For the rest of the day, Paul retold the story to anyone who would listen, killing his productivity for the day, and repeatedly asking anyone who would listen, "How could he possibly think that was okay?"

Judgment

One of our favorite pastimes as adults is people watching. Before Amazon and Target, we used to do this almost exclusively at shopping malls. We love to people watch at parks, in airports, on the internet, and yes, in shopping malls. People watching is a fascinating experience—mainly because people are fascinating! You never know what you're going to see when you indulge in a solid session of people watching. It gives us a great opportunity to make judgments about the people we watch. You don't need to admit it, but we've all seen an out-of-control kid and given our people-watching partner a sideways glance, as if to say, "This is going to be good" or "Where is that child's parent?" As human beings, we all love to judge. Judgment isn't necessarily bad or negative in nature, but it's important to recognize that we are making judgments.

Frequently the simple judgments we make arise from the dichotomies of good/bad or right/wrong. If we remember that our judgments are based on our perceptions and stories about the information (our interpretation), then we can catch our judgments and realize they are not as clearly rooted in reality as we believe them to be. With a different story comes a different judgment. You're at the zoo, for example, and you see a kid on a leash pulling his seemingly reluctant father through the trails just like a Labrador puppy. You decide he's a bad parent because he doesn't know how to watch his kid without leashing him up like a dog. Ordinarily, we don't gather enough information to tell a complete and accurate story. In this case, the story is that this father has no control over his kid and is not a good parent.

The information that we don't know is that this child has Restless Leg Syndrome and was in terrible pain sitting in the stroller. Because moving around is the best way for this boy to get relief, he often runs around without looking back. Last month, he was at the Aquarium on a busy day and was lost for two hours. His father was a wreck. Ever since then, they've used a backpack harness to allow him to get relief from his symptoms when they flare up, but also to keep him safe. Without all the information, we use our intuition and emotions to fill in the gaps. As soon as our story seems reasonable, the Illusion of Certainty shows up to remind us that we're right.

In fact, much of our misery comes from the stories we tell about the facts around us. For instance, imagine you're walking from one part of the office building to another and turn a corner down a fifty-foot long hallway. At the end of the hallway, someone turns the corner and starts walking toward you. You realize that it's a coworker you haven't seen for a few weeks. You call out an enthusiastic "Hello!" After taking two steps and making eye contact with you, she lets out an annoyed sigh, turns on her heel, and walks away from you. You're pretty sure she threw up her hands and muttered something as she turned.

What do you feel? What do you think? Many folks I've worked with have had similar experiences, and they're left feeling sad, confused, hurt, disappointed, or angry. "What did I do to piss her off?" they think to themselves. "She's in a mood. Well, that was rude." The story we often tell in this situation is that for some reason, she didn't want to interact with us.

Then, right before you leave for the night, you get an email from her. The subject line is, "SORRY!" The message reads, "I'm so sorry about not saying 'hi' in the hallway earlier. I was late for a meeting and realized that I didn't grab my notes off of the printer. I knew I was going to be late, so I ran back to get them as soon as I could."

If you've never had this experience, I guarantee you that someone you work with has. The stories that we tell ("She must be offended," "She's angry with me," "She's rude") are just that—stories. When you peel back the layers, trying to get to the facts, you're usually left with something much more benign: "She turned around." When you break down situations to return to your perceptions before they become colorized by your stories and judgments, you can see where you have an opportunity to choose how you feel and direct your ultimate reaction.

Often, we want to claim that we are at the mercy of our feelings, and therefore, other people can cause us to feel things. But when you understand the Perception Escalator, you realize that your feelings are under your control. In fact, the absurdity of this perception comes into sharp focus when we realize that we often say things the way kindergarteners do: "He hurt my feelings," or "He made me mad." That's simply not true. He didn't go into the center of my brain and fiddle with some neurons to trigger my feelings. My experience of feelings is based on my stories and judgments. I created my stories and judgments based on my perceptions.

Let's go back to your own kindergarten year to better explain my point. You're playing with your friends on the playground, and out of nowhere, POW, a big red rubber four-square ball hits you smack on the left side of your face. You don't quite fall down, but it hit you pretty hard. You can still hear the sound that the ball made when it bounced off of you. You immediately raise your left hand up to your face to try to stop the throbbing while looking around to see where that ball came from. Your friends point to Jackson, who's the only one in that direction. He's trying to avoid your eyes, but you can tell that he threw the ball at you and is hoping to not get in trouble. The next thing you know, your legs are running toward the nearest teacher so that you can tell on Jackson. "He kicked the ball at me on purpose, and he hurt my feelings!"

Your trip up the Perception Escalator went like this: I got hit by a ball in the face (Action). Jackson did it (Perception). Jackson did it on purpose (Story). Jackson did that because he's a mean kid (Judgment). He made me feel bad, sad, angry (Feelings). So I'm going to go tell the teacher and get him in trouble (Reaction). Here's the thing. We can't change what happened. Well, I'm the author, so I could do that, but in this scenario, what happens happens. Our first real opportunity to take control is with the story and the judgment.

Let's look at some alternative stories and judgments that we can make about this situation. Instead of "Jackson did it on purpose because he's a mean kid," maybe "Jackson's careless and did it by accident." Or maybe, "Jackson was trying to attract my attention because he's lonely and wants to play with me. Maybe *that's* why he was avoiding my eyes but kept looking in my direction." The latter two stories/judgments lead to sympathy and kindness rather than hurt feelings. Unfortunately, most people tend to believe that the stories that make us feel bad are true. Then we blame the villain in those stories for making us feel bad. But if we realize that we create the stories that cause those feelings, there is a much higher likelihood that we can avoid unnecessary upset.

To be clear, I'm not saying that people never do things that hurt you, or that being a victim is 100 percent your choice. I understand, personally, that that is not the case. The point I'm trying to illustrate is that we are often part of situations that cause ourselves (and other people) unnecessary suffering because of the judgment and story we create about information we don't know. This suffering is our fault because we choose the judgment and story.

Our friend Samantha in the break room was not reacting to the sign Karl posted or his request to clean the coffee pot. She was reacting to the perception, story, judgment, and feelings she experienced when she read the sign. By tearing down the sign, she reacted out of sheer frustration, genuinely believing that the sign made her feel that way. Many of us do the same thing when we're faced with a difference of opinion at work. We associate our feeling with the clearest cause, usually someone or their behavior. When our boss denies our request for a raise, we believe that she makes us feel bad.

But usually the feeling is caused by the story we tell ourselves that our boss doesn't think we deserve a raise. This reason for denying you a raise may or may not be true, but it's a story, nonetheless.

The lesson in the break room is that the sign did not make Samantha feel anger. She felt angry because she believed that the evening-shift people do not matter to the day-shift people. Karl's sign on the coffee pot was yet another example that reinforced her story. Just as we have the opportunity to tell different stories about Johnny on the playground, Samantha, too, could have told a different story and had a different feeling and reaction to Karl's request. For example, what if the story she told was that the break room is kept clean all day by the early-shift folks and ends up getting messy in the evenings, something that she's noticed before? What if she looked at that sign with empathy and decided she could chat with the rest of the night-shift folks to at least clean the coffee pot every night? If she told this story, her reaction would be completely different. She might even leave a friendly note of her own on the coffee pot.

When Karl walked into the break room and watched Samantha crumple up his note, he, too, told a story that didn't make him feel positive about the situation. This led to his immediate and aggressive response. If he told a different story, he, too, could have reacted with more empathy. He could have asked questions to try to understand Samantha and the rest of the late shift folks better. They could have worked together to draft a mutually beneficial plan. We always have an opportunity to tell different stories, and the impact can be powerful.

Why Did You Do That?

Your boss calls you in to his office and opens with, "Why did you do that?" in reference to a decision that you made the day before. As adults, we ask, "Why did you do that?" more often than we realize. But this question is not as straightforward as we believe it to be. An adult asking "Why?" is typically born of two motives. The first and most noble is curiosity—a genuine desire to understand the actions of another person. When you approach the question this way, you're assuming a lower power position as the learner, while the person you're asking becomes the person in a higher power position as the teacher.

The second motive for asking the question, "Why?" is born out of judgment. "Why would you do it that way?" The tone is different, and your goal is to put yourself in a higher position of power and authority. You are suggesting that you have the ability to critique the other person's work or decisions. The person being judged can choose to answer your pointed question and defend her actions or try to evade and ignore you. Beware of defensive behavior because it's a powerful influence on the middle steps of the Perception Escalator.

Our defensive behavior comes from the Acute Stress Response that we share with many other animals. The Acute Stress Response increases blood flow to our extremities so that we can respond effectively to a threat by running away as fast as possible or punching hard. This response is commonly called the Fight or Flight response.[15] When our body experiences the Fight or Flight response, our bodies sometimes feel jittery due to the production of adrenaline. We feel a buzz of energy due to our livers producing extra glucose. Animals, including humans, have developed this response so that we can survive threats and attacks. Remember, early humans had to survive saber-toothed tigers! According to the American Psychological Association, our defense mechanisms distort reality. They are means of coping with problems and external threats.[16] So when you notice that someone is reacting defensively to your "Why?" question, don't get offended. The person is not reacting to you—he's reacting to survival instincts programmed in his DNA. He's reacting to a saber-toothed tiger.

How do you keep people from reacting defensively and ensure that your motive for asking the question "Why?" comes from curiosity, rather than judgment? Well, remember that context has a lot to do with what someone perceives. If your words don't change ("Why did you do that?"), then all you can do is attempt to control or explain the context (and meaning) you create for yourself. Here are four ways that you can self-monitor context:

1. Monitor your internal monologue. If you are thinking, "You idiot!" "What a boneheaded move," "How could you possibly be so stupid?" that condescending context will likely shine through to the other person, even if you're trying to mask it from him.

2. Monitor your tone. Usually, if you have negative internal commentary going on, your tone will seem annoyed or exasperated. The context will betray you.

3. Monitor your face. Our facial expressions reveal a lot to people in our communications. If you are genuinely curious, the muscles in your face will take a more relaxed position, and your eyes will be inquisitive. If you are coming from a place of judgment, your face will be hardened because the question, "Why did you do that?" isn't exactly what you are trying to say. You are trying to make a statement (usually aligned with your internal commentary).

4. Monitor your body position. If you want to genuinely learn something new, put yourself in a receiving position. Sit back but be eager.

Also, please note that the context that the other person is operating from isn't all YOU. If the question, "Why did you do it that way?" comes after some mistake, she might start off from a defensive position and look for any and all critical attacks. In this case, monitor her context and make sure that you help put her in a place where she can perceive your true motives. As you ask your question, remember that the question is the Action step as she goes up her own Perception Escalator from there. What happens next will be based on the story that she tells and the judgment she makes of the situation. Monitor her reaction.

I Feel You

Stepping into another person's perspective is required if we are to imagine someone's journey up the Perception Escalator. We're talking here about empathy. Empathy is one of those topics that is so over-explained in leadership circles that it sounds funny if you say it too many times. Empathy empathy empathy empathy empathy empathy empathy empathy empathy. See what I mean? But I want to talk about empathy in a different way. Empathy has the ability to change us. When you break the word "empathy" down to its Greek origin it's "en" and "pathos," which means "in" and "feel." So empathy is actually being inside the feelings of another. Empathy is different from sympathy, which also has the same Greek root pathos but "syn" means "with." When we sympathize, we share someone else's feelings. When we empathize, we feel what someone else is feeling.

Unfortunately, many products are not created or designed with empathy. The designers do not get inside of the feelings of the end users. For example, on business trips when I check into a hotel in the late evening and make my way to my room, I usually start swiping and tapping the key card to get the door to open. I don't know why it never seems to open on the first try! (My history with hotels clearly triggers feelings.) I finally get the door to open, take a step inside, and either to my immediate right or to my immediate left is a light switch. Instinctively I'll flip the light switch, and in almost every hotel room, one single light bulb will turn on above my head. One Light! The rest of the room is still dark. To turn the lights on in the rest of the room, I'll have to go around to each individual lamp, one by one, and turn the little black knobs that usually scratch up my fingers. In fact, most of those lamps have three-way sockets, but with only one-way bulbs, so the first two turns don't work, and I end up turning the black knob over and over again. Eventually I'll think the light's not going to turn on, so I'll look over the lamp shade to see the bulb directly—just as it turns on, temporarily blinding me as if I'm in a slapstick comedy. Most hotel lighting is organized this way because the designers lack empathy for their customers' experience.

Functionally, hotel room lighting works this way for a couple of business-savvy reasons. Many hotels want a flexible design that enables them to rapidly change decor or remodel / modernize simply by replacing the lamps around the room. In addition, when architects design hotel rooms, they want to maximize living space and minimize space between rooms (including between floors), so they don't use overhead can lighting. Can lights and other overhead lights are a commonplace type of lighting in modern homes. In our homes, we're used to the lights coming on in a room when we flip a switch, so going through so many extra motions to get a hotel room bright can be infuriating.

Thankfully, not every hotel does this. I once stayed at a hotel in Spokane, Washington called the Davenport Grand that had recently been totally (and truly) remodeled. When I opened the door and flipped the light switch to my right, something amazing happened. The entire room brightened. This experience was so far out of the ordinary that, before I even put my bag down (and I'm going to sound like a total nerd here), I called my wife and told her about the light in this room. But the coolest thing happened when I went to bed that night. I reached over to the light switch next to the bed, flipped it, and the entire room went dark. This instant darkness struck me as incredible (I told you I'm a geek). "Now *these* hotel designers have empathy for guests!" I thought to myself. "They imagined what I would do and what I would need to make my hotel experience pleasant, comfortable, and easy." Amazing!

Similarly, Leatherman is a company that effectively empathizes with its customers who travel. The Leatherman is a multi-tool that many folks wear on their belt. If you open a Leatherman tool, it has pliers, knives, screwdrivers, scissors, etc. They're like Swiss Army knives but much more useful. Folks who carry the Leatherman love their Leatherman. Well, something started happening during the first decade of the TSA. Imagine that it's 2012, the eleventh year of the Transportation Security Administration, and you are going on a business trip. As you get to the TSA security area, you grab the bin and put in your phone and belt. With your trusty Leatherman safely tucked in the front pocket of your bag, you hoist it up on the conveyer belt and make your way through security screening. As you wait for your bag and bin on the other side of the x-ray machine, the TSA agent calls out, "Whose bag is this?" You look up and to your dismay, it's your bag. "Great. . ." you think sarcastically. "Just what I need."

The TSA agent takes your bag to the bag time-out table and asks before unzipping it, "Is there anything sharp that could hurt my hand?" You say, "My Leatherman is in there, but it's in its nylon case." The TSA agent thanks you and, looking at the monitor seems to confirm that's what she's looking for. She unzips your bag and pulls out the black case that holds your Leatherman. She says, "I'm sorry, but this cannot be carried onto the plane. You need to check it." Considering that you have already checked your suitcase and that your laptop and book are in your carry-on bag, you don't want to check it; your only choice is to allow them to confiscate it. As you walk away from the security area, you see the TSA agent take your beloved Leatherman and lock it away in a drawer. How do you feel?

According to Leatherman CEO Ben Rivera, this scenario happened to many people. Folks who had their Leatherman taken away started calling and writing emails to Leatherman customer service, explaining how they felt. One day, Mr. Rivera was denied entry to the Disneyland Theme Park because of the Leatherman that he put in his bag. All at once, he felt what his customers felt. In an interview with online newspaper SNEWS, Rivera said, "I knew there had to be a way to create a truly useful tool that you could take past security. I came home from that trip, I started working on TREAD right away."

The Leatherman Tread is a wristband with links, and each link has a set of tools. You can customize the tools on your wristband, and you can even buy a watch face for it. The designers at Leatherman empathized with their users, understood their experience, and designed something that fit the needs of their users. To see a photo of the Leatherman Tread, go to www.EricMBailey.com/leatherman.

When we empathize, it does something to the way we think, feel, or perceive a situation. For example, let's say that you're joining your coworker Alex for lunch during an out of town business trip, but he shows up fifteen minutes late. If you're like most people, you feel a little annoyed at his tardiness. But what if he calls you thirty minutes prior to the scheduled meeting time and tells you that he's lost and hasn't been able to follow the directions *you* gave him? There was at least one wrong turn, bad landmark references, and the distances seemed inaccurate. How do you feel then? Typically, you might be pleasantly surprised that he's *only* fifteen minutes late, given the circumstances. And you'll probably apologize for making it hard on him to find the location. You'll also understand what it took for him to get there. You'll understand the inadequate tools he had to work with—your directions. Rather than criticizing him, you'll empathize with him. This empathy makes forgiveness and understanding so much easier. The word empathy has been used so much in a leadership context, that it's almost cliché. But this change in ease of understanding and forgiveness is the real reason that empathy is important. True empathy changes your judgments. This Transformation of Empathy is the sixth Principle of Human Understanding.

When we are at work and someone fails to meet our expectations, how quickly do we jump in to judge them harshly for not being able to produce what we expected? What if, instead, we practice empathy, stepping inside their experience and their feelings, understanding the tools they have to work with? We would change our judgments, as well as our own emotions and reactions to them. That shift is the real reason for leaders and managers to be empathetic. When we step inside the experiences and the feelings of the people who work with us, we judge them less harshly, and they are subsequently quicker to improve their performance.

In their 2016 research, Ilka Gleibs, Neil Wilson, Geetha Reddy, and Caroline Catmur explore "Automatic Imitation"—how during interactions when you believe you are in the same social group as someone else, and you expect a collaborative interaction, you will actually mirror some of the other person's physical behaviors. If she nods her head, you will subtly nod your head. If she smiles, you will smile. These mirrored behaviors unconsciously communicate understanding and connectedness. These actions indicate to the person that you are feeling what she is feeling.

On the television show *Brain Games*, the host, modern philosopher and futurist, Jason Silva, presented an experiment based on Automatic Imitation, which showed how the perception of empathy can cause positive feelings. When we believe people empathize with us and understand us, it changes the way we feel about them. Silva's experiment involved a computer-generated face on a monitor with a camera on top of the screen, similar to a webcam one would use for videoconferencing. Human test subjects were instructed to talk to the face on the screen. The face was actually controlled by an actor in another room with facial tracking sensors and computer software. Whatever the actor did, so did the face on the monitor. In the first part of the experiment, the actor would use the camera to watch the facial movements of the test subject as they told a story. He would then either delay or make the opposite facial expressions of the human test subject. When the subjects would smile or nod their head up and down, the face on the screen would frown or shake side to side.

In the second part of the experiment, the face on the screen imitated the head nods and facial expressions of the test subject. When the subjects got animated and raised their eyebrows, so did the face on the screen. When the subjects would laugh and bounce their heads up and down, so would the face on the screen. After the experiment, all the test subjects were asked to relay how they felt about the two faces. When reporting on the face that mimicked their expressions and feelings, they said things like, "I liked the first one. It felt like he understood me." When they related how they felt about the second instance, they said things like, "It seemed very robotic," or "It was a little rude," or "It was cold."

When the test subjects felt as though the robot empathized with them, they felt a kinship with it, associating human feelings and emotions with a mechanical object. They even kept using the pronoun "he" rather than "it," and showed affinity for the face, simply because they felt that the robot understood them. These responses demonstrate that as human beings, we have a desire to be understood. When we sense that people empathize with us, it changes our experience with them. Empathy has a transformational power to change both our judgments of other people, and other people's judgments of us.

An excellent excerpt from Benjamin Franklin's autobiography talks about the significant effects of using empathy in relationships. I have paraphrased from the original Eighteenth-Century King's English:

> I make it a rule not to directly oppose the opinions of others and assert my own opinions. I've even forbidden myself from using absolutes or words of absolute opinion, such as "certainly," "undoubtedly," etc. Instead, I use phrases like, "I believe," "I gather," "It seems to me that," "It appears to me that."
>
> When someone shared something, I thought was wrong, I denied myself the pleasure of jumping in to oppose them, showing the flaw in their thinking. As I responded to them, I began by realizing that in a different situation, their opinion would be correct, just not in the current circumstance.
>
> I soon found the advantage of this change. The conversations that I had were more pleasant. The modest way that I offered my opinions found them met with a better reception and less opposition. I was less embarrassed when I was found to be wrong, and others were more open to admitting mistakes and joining me, if I happened to be right.
>
> And even though this change was against my natural instinct at first, it has become so easy and habitual for me, that perhaps for the past fifty years, no one has ever heard an absolute from my mouth. After my character of integ-

rity, I think that it is because of this habit, that I have had so much influence over my fellow citizens when I propose new ideas or changes to old ideas. I would say that I was a bad speaker. I'm not eloquent, I hesitate while choosing the right words, often use the wrong words, and yet, my points generally carried the day.

Principles of Human Understanding

The Observation Trap Principles

Can trap us by influencing the way we observe the world.

1. The Illusion of Certainty
2. Perception is More Important Than Reality
3. The Desire to Fight to Be Right
4. The Power of Distinction
5. Context is the Underlying Fabric by Which We Encounter the World
6. Empathy Changes Your Judgment

CHAPTER 3

Understanding Bias

"We find comfort in those who agree with us;
growth in those who don't."

–Frank Clark

Whenever I introduce the topic of bias, some people become uncomfortable. I notice people repositioning themselves in their chairs as if they are hunkering down in preparation for an incoming attack. I have interviewed several folks about why they have this physical reaction, and they say something to the effect of, "Because bias is bad. It's uncomfortable." When I dig a little deeper, they explain to me that they believe that bias is equal to racism, and racism is bad, so therefore, bias is bad. Then occasionally I hear the instantaneous, almost unconscious statement, "I am not biased." The problem with the belief that "bias is bad" is that it's inaccurate.

According to the Psychologist Kendra Chery, bias is a systematic error in thinking that impacts our judgments and decisions.[17] Think about when you were a kid, just barely tall enough to reach up and touch the stove. You're not tall enough yet to see the stove, but you know that your mom and dad spend a lot of time touching things up there. You go to reach up, and your dad says, "No! That's hot!" so you back away—for now. Your curiosity grows with every passing minute that you don't know what's up there. As soon as your dad is gone, you toddle over to the stove, reach up and feel the cool metal of the surface, bring your hand to the right and, "YEOWWCH!" In an instant, you understand what "hot" means. But guess what? The neurons inside your brain make many more connections than that. The throbbing, burning pain in your hand has created a new fear of the stove. You now understand that stove equals danger, and you should steer clear of the stove.

Recall that "bias" is a systematic error in thinking that impacts our judgments and decisions. Because of this incident, you decide that stoves should be avoided because they are hot and dangerous. But that error in thinking is keeping you safe—it therefore can't be bad. In fact, it's *not* bad; it just exists. Moreover, bias born of experience is part of what has made us human beings successful as a species. We can rapidly, almost instinctively, identify danger and survive. We can recognize potential threats and make decisions, a trait that has evolved to ensure we thrive.

If you were lost in the wilderness of coastal Oregon, and it had been days since you had seen any food or clean water, but then your tired body came across a bush full of unfamiliar red berries, would you eat them? (I'm assuming that you are like most people and are thinking an emphatic, "NO!") Hundreds of generations ago, when we were hunter-gatherers, many of us tried to eat red berries and, unfortunately, perished. The rest of us learned that red berries might be dangerous. So we started to make associations between red berries and danger. The error in our thinking occurs when we assume that all red berries are poisonous and instinctively avoid them—which makes strawberry farmers berry unhappy! As it turns out, the red berries that you avoided in Oregon were barberries and are good for heart health and acne. But our learned bias against red berries has kept us thriving as a species! Therefore, bias is not bad in and of itself. What's important to understand is that bias exists and that it's an evolutionary trait used to create understanding through patterns. Bias exists in all of us—and for good reason!

Now consider how perception and bias interact through the lens of our lives. We perceive the world, and then we run what we perceive through the filters of our past experience and learnings. We judge a situation by expecting a pattern, and finally, we decide what to do. Sometimes these judgments and patterns are influenced by deliberate training. If you're giving a presentation and you see the CEO fold her arms, you remember from communication training that when a person folds her arms, it means that she is closed off. Your confidence is shaken because, all of a sudden, you perceive that your CEO is closed off to what you are presenting.

Other times our judgments and patterns are influenced by emotions sparked by our past experiences. You have been working for your boss for two years now and have not yet been given a raise. Your friends keep telling you to go to him and ask for it, but you refuse because you believe that it's a waste of time. You have asked each of your previous three bosses for raises and were denied each time for one reason or another, so you perceive that you are not worthy of a raise.

Understanding the Truth About Bias is the seventh of the twenty-two Principles of Human Understanding. Bias, along with all the other principles, is universal to all humans. This means that there are two ways to apply the knowledge so that we can: (1) understand ourselves better and choose when and where to let these processes control us and (2) understand other human beings better and why they behave irrationally.

Fundamental Attribution Error (FAE)

Let's talk about the Fundamental Attribution Error. The American Psychological Association defines "Fundamental Attribution Error" as the tendency to overestimate the relationship between someone's behavior and their character and underestimate the relationship between their behavior and the circumstance.[18] The phrase "Fundamental Attribution Error" is a mouthful of scary-sounding psychology jargon that couldn't hold your attention longer than this seemingly long sentence. So instead, let's just talk about "FAE."

FAE is a tricky phenomenon that plagues us every day. FAE happens when you look at your phone and realize that you lost track of time responding to emails, and the meeting is starting in two minutes. Unfortunately, your office is a five-minute walk from the conference room. You grab your notebook and a pen and dash down the hallway, up the stairs, just slowing your pace before you come into view of the conference room's glass windows. You stride in two minutes late but take your seat as Alice is introducing the agenda. You're so proud of yourself for making it and not being out of breath.

Five minutes later, Frank conspicuously opens the door to the conference room and, out of breath, takes a seat at the back of the room. He sprawls his wad of loose papers onto the table and his pen, which was tucked inside the papers, rolls onto the floor. Everybody looks. "At least I wasn't *that* late," you think to yourself. "Frank is always running into meetings late. That guy is so disorganized!"

Most people in this situation think something derogatory along these lines, assigning his tardiness to a flaw in his character. Now here's the crazy thing. Remember the behavior you exhibited immediately before judging Frank for walking into the meeting late? You were late! FAE occurs when two people have a similar problem, like showing up late to a meeting. We are quick to judge another person and attribute his problem to something wrong in his character, but when we look at ourselves in the same situation, rather than blame ourselves, we blame our external surroundings, like we had an overwhelming number of emails, or the elevator was too slow, or someone stopped to talk to us. The eighth Principle of Human Understanding is that Fundamental Attribution Error (FAE) is all around us. It is so ubiquitous and influential in our communication and relationships that we need to monitor it as we attempt to collaborate.

Here's another example. Remember the story about Paul driving in to work? Paul judges the driver of the big black diesel truck as unkind, unsafe, and rude. Paul said, "He's a maniac with obvious anger issues!" He attributes the poor driving to a flaw in the driver's character. Paul is making a judgment about that driver based on limited information. He is identifying problems in the driver's behavior (driving too fast, driving on the shoulder). Then he attributes the problems to some flaw in the driver's character: "He has no regard for human life."

Think about how frustrated you would be in that situation. Do you jump to tell a more complete story of the person, inventing a reasonable explanation for his behavior? Or do you experience a flare of emotion (fear, anger, or hurt) and react with a horn blast and a mono-digital salute? In most cases, we don't know the reality of the other person's situation—the real reason the person is driving that way. All we can do is invent a story. FAE helps us invent a story that they are an *$&#0@3. They are reckless and inconsiderate. We judge their character.

Ironically, if Paul himself ever drove in a similar hurried fashion, he wouldn't say he was driving fast because he had no regard for human life. Instead, he would say something like he had to drive fast because his alarm didn't go off, or because he got stuck behind a huge traffic jam and he was late, or any infinite number of external excuses. If you've ever had an employee who was routinely late to work, you know the full litany of reasons. None of the reasons ever seem to be, "It was my fault."

This is where the Perception Escalator comes in. What we've done is create stories in which Frank and the other driver are villains (antagonists) to us, the protagonist. Why don't we, instead, invent a story that makes us feel less negative about our coworker Frank or the other driver? If we understand that our natural inclination is to make the other person a villain, whether or not it's true, then we can just as easily make her a hero.

Try this: Any time you have a driver aggressively pass you or cut you off in traffic, consider saying, "I hope she makes it to the hospital in time!" If a coworker comes in late to a meeting, think to yourself, "I'll bet he was late because one of his kids was sick, and he had to scramble to figure out what to do." By considering positive explanations for someone else's behavior, a couple of wonderful things will happen: (1) You will let go of the frustration of the situation much sooner than if you hold on to the angry story of the villain; (2) You will remember him later in the day and find yourself wondering if he worked things out all right, hoping the best for him! You'll find that thinking in these positive ways creates a much better situation than retelling the same awful stories to anyone you can get to listen.

FAE Is Water Torture for Relationships

When you think about what FAE does for our relationships, think of the person who is always complaining about their coworkers. Every time you talk with John, he goes on and on about what an "unqualified coworker" did or a "lazy coworker" didn't do. *The FAE is strong with this one.* The first couple of times it happens you listen to John, maybe even agreeing with him on a point or two, offering your own examples to show you agree and reinforce his opinion. Then, after a while, you realize a pattern, and you think to yourself, "Yeah, complaining about people I work with isn't the way I want to spend my days. I need to do something about this."

One day, you subtly bring up the issue to Wendy over lunch. "Have you noticed that John always talks bad about other people?"

"Yeah!" she exclaims, clearly waiting to talk with someone about this. "It's as if he has to point out and attack every little mistake someone makes."

"Thank you! I'm so glad I'm not the only one who sees it."

"I think he's got some real insecurity he's dealing with," she says. "I mean, John, you've been here for fifteen years! Relax. You're set!'"

"The worst part is that every time he talks to me about someone, all I can think about is how he's probably talking bad about me to other people." Finally, with exasperation, you side with Wendy. "He's just such a negative person."

And FAE strikes again. In fact, FAE has been present in all John's conversations when he attributes anything wrong with the characters of his coworkers rather than paying attention to their situation. And then (did you notice?) FAE also became present when you and Wendy started talking ABOUT John: "He attacks people." "He's insecure." "He's such a negative person." With your coworker over lunch, you were talking about how John lets FAE get in the way even while both of you let FAE get in the way for yourselves. Imagine if the entire team lets FAE control our conversations and our beliefs. What do you think happens to communication? To collaboration? To productivity?

As you see, FAE can be a very strong influence on our perceptions and our judgments. That's why we want to catch FAE whenever it's present and check our judgments about another person's character against reality. This is important because the Illusion of Certainty will make you believe that your judgment is, in fact, correct. When you notice that you're going down the path of judgment, it's imperative that you recognize FAE might be trying to squeeze into your conversation.

My first chance to be a boss was working for a concessions company for which we popped and sold Kettle Korn at the Phoenix Zoo. I swear, I can still smell the caramelized sugar that burned into my forearms. The owner of the company, Scott Grondin, took me under his wing and taught me his philosophy of management. Scott is still a mentor of mine to this day. He always assumed the best in people. One day, he was teaching me about reordering and stock levels, when he got a call on his cell phone. It was an employee who was scheduled to be at work fifteen minutes earlier. We employed mostly high-school and college-aged kids, so I knew what the call was going to be about. When Scott picked up the phone, he didn't even give her a chance to give her excuse for being late. "Hey," he said. "It's good to hear from you. Is everything okay?" Obviously, Scott's concern rather than criticism for this employee caught her off guard. She said yes and apologized, telling him she'd be there in about five minutes.

I asked Scott about why he handled the phone call this way. Because in every single job that I had ever worked at, calling about being late was either an exercise in creative storytelling, selling, or a con job—or maybe all three. It didn't make sense to me why he didn't run her through the wringer for being late. His response landed deep in my heart and has never left. "She expects to be taken to task," he said, "so she's going to lie or exaggerate excuses. That doesn't do us any good. She's already on her way, so I would rather have her arrive, knowing that I care about her, than arrive thinking that she's in trouble. She will likely remember the kindness and not want to be late again. Best-case scenario, she remembers the kindness and passes it along to someone when she's a manager." When we remove FAE like Scott did, it seems anything is possible.

My friend Randy calls this concept "Presumed Benevolence." When we practice Presumed Benevolence, we PRESUME that the actions or behaviors of a person are inspired by good rather than negative intentions. In other words, instead of assuming a selfish or erroneous motivation, we choose to imagine a noble intent. Like Scott, when you see your employee Jackie come to work late, rather than presuming she's irresponsible, you could presume that she intended to arrive on time but had some challenge you know nothing about.

Assuming negative motivation is becoming a larger and larger problem in our society. Remember when you were texting back and forth with your friend and she went radio silent for a while? In that time, what did you presume? For most people, after an extended period of time, the presumption is negative. Often, your first thought is, "I must have said something wrong. She's mad at me" (story). The perception is that because she was texting back and forth for so long but then stops suddenly, something must have changed. The change must be that she was engaged, but then something took her out of the conversation. "It must have been something I wrote," you think. "Let me read and reread the last several messages to see what I said to offend her." Then you really get agitated when you make up some reason that she must be upset and still hasn't texted you back. "Why would she get offended by that? That doesn't make any sense. Geeze, she's too sensitive" (FAE).

Back in the break room when Samantha walked in, what did she see? She saw a sign that read: Please don't be an animal! Clean and rinse the coffee maker after 4:00 p.m." After reading the sign, she perceived an attack on who she was personally. Then FAE showed up, and Samantha believed that whoever wrote this sign must be selfish and inconsiderate. It drove her to stand up for herself and the rest of the late-shift team.

What did Karl see when he walked into the break room? He saw Samantha taking down his sign. He presumed that her action was a physical manifestation of her disrespect and lack of appreciation for him personally. FAE kicked right in, and he made the judgment that Samantha was a mean person. He witnessed her tearing down his sign. He might have even perceived a devilish smile on her face, which may have enraged Karl. It's possible that Samantha didn't smile as she was taking down the sign, but that doesn't matter. Karl perceived it, and he based his journey up the Perception Escalator on the idea that she ripped down the sign and smiled about it.

The path to presumptions and making up negative stories is easy for us to follow. Here's how the path works and where it can lead: "Perception" of behavior can trigger FAE, which gets cemented by the Illusion of Certainty, which can lead to arguments, frustration, and damaged relationships at work, at home, or between friends. If you want to practice maintaining good relationships everywhere in your life, stay open to the possibility of another person's positive intent or reasonable explanation.

Availability Heuristic: What You Know → How You Know It

Please build a picture in your mind of the following person: I am a librarian. I am forty-five-years old. I wear glasses. I have blond hair. I am about five feet, six inches tall. I have worked for the past twelve years at the front desk of my local library. I usually wear brown shoes, tan pants, and one of several library T-shirts. My name is Stephan.

If you're like most people, the image you created in your mind of this librarian changed dramatically when I introduced the final fact—the librarian's name. Some of you reading the words on the page may have even perceived his name as "Stephanie" because the male name "Stephan" was so far outside the image of a librarian being built in your head. When I do this exercise in person with leadership groups, I've even had people tell me that I have a typo in the description: "Ummm, Eric, you forgot the 'ie' on the end of Stephanie, the librarian's name."

"Thank you so much for the feedback," I say, "but I think that it is you who is *adding* 'ie' to Stephan, the librarian's name."

The reason most of us imagine a blonde woman rather than a blonde man is a concept called "Availability Heuristic." According to the *APA Dictionary of Psychology*, "Availability Heuristic" is a mental shortcut we use to accelerate decision-making. Essentially, if we can recall something readily available to our memory, we are more likely to build our decisions from that memory. Since most of our lives we've known mostly female librarians and would be hard-pressed to think of a male librarian, our mental model only (or mostly) has available memories of female librarians. As we began to build our image of the librarian described in this example, we unconsciously started with a female template. Then we added the hair, the glasses, the shoes, etc.

The Availability Heuristic plays out for us all the time, and usually, it's benign. But I've witnessed recent examples that had more impact. The first example occurred when I overheard a person arrive at a leadership conference. Walking up to the check-in table, he said, "Hi, I'm sorry I'm late. My boss will be joining us shortly."

"Oh, good, what's his name?"

After a pause, he responded, "Um, *her* name is Pamela."

The second example occurred when a medical emergency occurred on my flight from Phoenix to Seattle. As I waited in line for the lavatory, a woman walked to the back and said she was dizzy. I grabbed her elbow and asked if she needed help.

She responded slowly, "I think I'm passing out." As soon as I moved behind her to help, she fell backwards in my arms, and I laid her down on the ground. I asked the person in the last seat to push the call button. Unfortunately, that person was a Chinese tourist who didn't speak English and had no idea what I was asking her to do. Eventually, we flagged a flight attendant who ran back to us. Picking up the intercom, the flight attendant asked, "Would any medical professionals or first responders, please come to the back of the plane?"

The first person to the back was a woman who happened to be sitting in my row. She probably got to the back first because my seat was empty, and she didn't have to crawl over anyone. When she got to the back, the flight attendant asked, "Ma'am, are you a nurse?"

"No, I'm a doctor," she responded matter-of-factly, without making any eye contact.

In this case, of course, our brains are more likely to recall (have available) recurring images of male doctors. In fact, if you do a Google image search for "doctor," you'll find that fewer than 17 percent of the images feature a female doctor. In reality, according to data from the Kaiser Family Foundation, more than one third of physicians in the United States are female.[19]

Human susceptibility to the Availability Heuristic is not necessarily a bad thing. Yes, it can lead us to some incorrect conclusions, but our brains have developed this and other heuristics so that we can rapidly identify patterns to make quick sense of the world around us. I don't believe the flight attendant was intentionally being sexist. She was in a stressful situation and tried to get the information that mattered most to her: "Is this person a qualified medical professional?" Remember the "Find the F's" exercise from Chapter 1? I introduced the concept that our brains take shortcuts under stress. While her intention was to obtain information, under stress, her brain took the shortcut of Female + Medical Professional = Nurse.

Likewise, when early human beings came upon red berries thousands of years ago, as they analyzed whether or not to eat them, they referred to previous information that red berries were dangerous. Accordingly, they chose not to eat the berries. These heuristics are not necessarily bad. They are simply present in us, and our brains often rely heavily on them—with good reason. If we become more conscious of them, we can choose to act on them or reconsider their influence on our decisions.

Trust Me, I'm from the Midwest

Imagine that Mike is on a spring break family vacation in beautiful Phoenix, Arizona. Mike decides to take his family to one of the dozens of daily Major League Baseball Spring Training games hosted in the Phoenix area. While they're seated on the general admission lawn in left field of Scottsdale Stadium watching the Giants take on the Mariners, his kids start asking, "What's for dinner?"

"I don't know," he says, pulling up Google Maps on his phone. "What kind of food do you want?"

His three kids and his wife start talking over one another, but the overwhelming favorite: tacos! Just then, a man seated on the lawn a few feet to their right says in a thick Minnesotan accent, "I heard you talkin' about tacos. You've gotta try the Barrio Queen place in Scottsdale. They have amazing tortillas, don'cha know." Mike chuckles to himself because the man grossly mispronounces "tortillas" as "tore-till-uhs."

And based on the butting in and that gross mispronunciation, do you think Mike trusts the recommendation of this guy? Would you? Of course not.

"Thanks, eavesdropping dude from Minnesota," Mike thinks to himself, "but we're going to find our own taco place."

Now, the fact is, the man with the Minnesotan accent happens to be correct—Barrio Queen *does* have amazing tortillas. But Mike doesn't trust him because he has neither earned nor been granted authority in Mike's decision-making. In fact, his mispronunciation of the word "tortilla," a word that's critical to good tacos, undermines any credibility that he might have had in Mike's mind.

Here's a different scenario: Mike and his family go on summer vacation to Madrid, Spain. They're on the Madrid metro, one of the most complex train systems in the world. With its 182 miles of track throughout the city and its 1,700 escalators, the metro can be pretty confusing. This is day three of their vacation, so the constant tapestry of Castilian Spanish is starting to sound both beautiful and extra confusing. Mike and his family are sitting on the semi-comfortable train seats, looking at both the oversized train system map and the city destinations map trying to figure out where they are and where they're going, when they hear the most amazing sound from behind them—an American accent! (Substitute your country of origin here, and you'll have a similar experience.) Mike's head whips around as he tries to identify the source. It's a guy seated a couple of rows away from Mike and his family. Mike tries his best to make eye contact as the man is talking with what appears to be his daughter. As soon as Mike catches the man's eye, he mouths the question, "American?"

With a big beaming smile on his face, the man says, "Yes" and waves Mike over. Then Mike starts sharing his story about how he's on vacation with his family, and they've gotten a little lost.

"We're on vacation, too—from Minnesota," the man says. "My daughter is considering going to school here." Then the man tells Mike, "Yesterday, we ate at this wonderful tapas restaurant and had the most amazing food." Mike chuckles a bit as he notices that the attempt to pronounce the Spanish word "tapas" is a little off. The man notices Mike's oversized map and reorients it. "I think that it's. . . yes, there it is. It's right here." The man says excitedly. "In fact, if you get off on the next stop, it's only a two-block walk." Mike looks toward his family with a happy grin because he knows exactly where his family will be going to dinner. Mike trusts the recommendation of this guy. The funny thing is, this could very well be the *same* guy Mike met in Phoenix!

Why did Mike trust this guy in Spain, but he didn't trust him in Phoenix? In other words, who granted him authority in Spain, but not in Phoenix? Mike did—and why? The main reason most Americans will trust another American when they're traveling abroad is because of tribalism. In Spain, that American guy from Minnesota is part of Mike's tribe. In Phoenix, he's just another guy. Let's explore this deeper.

Birds of a Feather Flock Together

In his 2006 book, *Globalism, Nationalism, Tribalism: Bringing Theory Back In,* Professor Paul James defines tribalism as the "accumulation of practices and meanings of identity, practically assumed or self-consciously effected."[20] Essentially, tribalism is the experience of humans organizing into groups. The word "tribe" is often used to indicate groups of native peoples. In my own book, I will be using the words "tribe" and "tribalism" to describe the underlying brain science that formed those groups and that holds them so powerfully together. This is the same brain science that makes it natural for us to create groups so that we can easily understand Us (the in-group) and Not-Us (the out-group).

In fact, tribalism is another one of the reasons that we've survived as a species. As with other evolutionary advantages, our brains release chemicals to let us know that we're doing a good thing. In the case of meeting someone from our own tribe, our brains release oxytocin. Oxytocin is a hormone released when we trust and our trust is rewarded. In other words, if we trust in the goodness of someone or something (and that something doesn't turn out to hurt or kill us), our brain releases a chemical that helps us form bonds, increase romantic attraction, build empathy, and lower depression. Have you ever had a perfect trip with a fantastic driver using a ride-sharing app? He talks just the right amount—not too much and not too little, with music playing at the perfect volume, and no offensive body odor. Whenever you get into someone else's car, you are trusting them with your safety and transportation needs. If the driver is fantastic, and the trip is safe, when you leave the car, you actually experience a wave of good feeling. That's oxytocin.

This no-trust/trust chemical release process is how we have developed societies. Back when we were cavewomen and cavemen, we had to put ourselves in vulnerable positions every night. In a world where everything was a potential threat, being unconscious for hours was not ideal. We started to organize into tribes so that while we slept, nobody would come and steal our rabbit meat. First, I would sleep, and you would keep watch; then you would sleep, and I would keep watch. Every time we trusted one another and our trust was rewarded (by nothing bad happening), our brains would release oxytocin. From those humble beginnings, we have used our tribes and tribal thinking to create roads that cross just about every country on the planet. Because of tribes, we know who is Us and who is Not-Us. This thinking brings community and validation to members inside the group, but also creates alienation for those outside the group.

Silos—Not Just for Grain Anymore

In agriculture, bulk grain is stored in large cylindrical storage containers called silos. While there are many different styles of silos, the most common are several thirty- to fifty-foot cylinders made of metal or concrete standing next to one another. To better regulate the conditions of the grain, each silo is designed to use relatively little ground surface area.

Similarly, through a modern type of tribalism at work, people often organize into silos. Tribalism at work is a powerful force that turns organizations into disparate divisions of micro organizations, all competing for the same resources. Rather than a unified team (Us), we turn into "Our Department" and "The Other Departments." We even start to identify "those other people," who tend to behave in the same way.

One of the best examples of tribalism at work is the opinion that "HR is the enemy." During my three years as an organizational development professional in the human resources department for a health-care firm, I heard this point of view toward HR dozens of times. In a typical business, the human resources department is responsible for, among other things, ensuring that the organization adheres to all the labor laws, protecting the organization from costly mistakes and lawsuits. Often, this responsibility means members of the HR team (silo) must say no to potentially risky decisions.

Over time, the HR team begins to gain a reputation as "The Enforcers" or "The NO Team." I've even heard employees in HR called "Joy Killers" and "Fun Police." In response, the HR team slowly turns inward for moral support, while the rest of the organization begins to attempt to shield itself from the HR team. A clear "Us" versus "Them" division begins to form. As a former HR team member, I'm not *even* going to go into the emotional heartache of never being invited to happy hour or birthday celebrations because I'll probably just end up crying on the keyboard. These kinds of divisions exist in many organizations. For example, nonphysical (but felt) boundaries can get created between "finance" and "accounting." Or the physical boundaries between executives located in a separate wing or level of the building from other employees reinforce the perception of "Us" versus "Them."

Once again, I'm not saying that tribalism is necessarily bad. I just want to illustrate that it exists. Human beings naturally build divisions of Us and Not-Us. We feel more comfortable when we are members of a group with a common goal—or a common enemy (#BeatLA). However, it's also common to berate members of the group who come "late" to our tribe when something goes well—those annoying "bandwagon fans." For example, I'm originally from the Seattle area in Washington. In 2014, when the Seattle Seahawks won the Super Bowl, fan support for the team exploded. One thing that surprised me was seeing the number of people who discounted the qualifications of some of these "new" fans, as if people didn't deserve to cheer for the team because they hadn't cheered for an arbitrary minimum number of years before the Seahawks were good.

I personally felt the pressure so strongly that I often found myself describing the length of time that I had been a Seahawks fan by naming my favorite players from when I was a kid, trying to earn my credentials as a "true Seahawks fan." Now that I've experienced this "real fan" type of tribalism, I see it all the time with the fans of the Golden State Warriors, the Houston Astros, or any sports team that wins a championship. I see it with fans of bands that make it big. I even see it with fans of tech brands like Apple or Tesla. I'm not saying that there aren't bandwagon fans who get excited about the team's success and only then actively cheer for the team because there are those types of fans. But why does that make "true fans" upset? Isn't it better to have more people cheering for your team than fewer? Isn't it ideal for the team to have more fans? Why, then, do we push people out of the tribe? Folks who are upset about bandwagon fans feel like those fans have not earned the right to call themselves fans. "True fans" believe that "bandwagon fans" are not die-hard fans who struggled through the bad times. They're just opportunists, only here to enjoy the good times.

Like "true fans," we will frequently identify qualifications within our tribes. Sometimes, it just makes us feel better if our tribes are more exclusive. The "Seahawks Fan" tribe becomes two distinct tribes: "Real Seahawks Fans" and "Bandwagon Seahawks Fans." In this way, the boundaries of our tribes are fluid. They can be modified by the perceptions of the members. As we create these new boundaries, we are intentionally keeping people outside our group. When you think about how often we create these kinds of groups—not just in sports, but at work—the phenomenon can be alarming, especially for leaders paying any attention to employee engagement and retention or their organization's morale and productivity from individuals and teams. The Fluidity of Tribal Boundaries is the ninth Principle of Human Understanding.

In Samantha's case, tribal association is strong for her because she has clearly differentiated the late-shift folks from the rest of the employees. The late-shift folks share the same schedule, but more than that, they share the same conversation after all the other people go home. If you were to walk into the breakroom after 5:00 p.m., you would regularly hear the following comments: "Day-shift people don't understand us." "Nobody cares about us." "People don't get how vital our work is to the organization." And "If it weren't for us, this whole place would grind to a halt." Have you ever said something like that? Have you ever participated in conversations like that? Most likely you have, because it isn't just a late-shift conversation—it's a common workplace hushed conversation.

For Samantha and the rest of the late-shift employees, these conversations reinforced the tribal boundaries of late-shift employees versus everyone else. This boundary made it significantly easier for her to perceive "them" launching yet another attack by posting that sign. Karl and Samantha work for the same company, ultimately wanting the same success for the organization. Yet they see themselves in two different tribes. They are behaving just like the "Real Seahawks Fans" and the "Bandwagon Seahawks Fans."

Psychologists define the "Bandwagon Effect" as the subtle compulsion to have more affinity towards something if and when other people show preference for that thing. The phrase originally comes from parades that had floats with a band playing on them, encouraging people to jump onto the float and dance. The more people that would jump on the float and dance, the more people wanted to jump on the float and dance. The Bandwagon Effect is something that marketers have used for decades to influence buying behavior: "Over 1 Billion sold. . . ," "America's Most Trusted. . . ," "Everyone has a. . . ."

When you think about the practical impacts of the Bandwagon Effect, you see the genesis of an organizational culture filled with gossip or complaining. You also see the reasoning behind the compulsory action of pulling out your phone when someone near you pulls out their phone. This also explains why so many people own but have never read *The Da Vinci Code*. When a book hits a bestseller list, more people buy it, and a portion of those people never actually get around to reading the book. But because it was a "bestseller," meaning there's measurable proof that many people have bought (and presumably read) the book, that must mean the book is good. That being said, thank you so much for buying and reading my book!

The Bandwagon Effect is sometimes called the "Lemming Effect." Many people believe that lemmings (adorable little gerbil-looking creatures) will follow the group no matter what. If one lemming jumps off a cliff, for example, the rest of the members of the group will follow the leader and hurl themselves off the cliff to their deaths. Now, because I like to dispel myths and misconceptions, I want to tell you that lemmings do not hurl themselves off of cliffs. This belief about lemming behavior (a perception) came about through a 1958 Academy Award winning documentary-style nature film produced by Disney. The film, *White Wilderness*, depicted hundreds of lemmings hurling themselves off a cliff into the Arctic Sea, ultimately to their deaths. An authoritative voice-over narrator described the inexplicable behavior of animals voluntarily ending their lives. The narrator offered a couple of suggestions as to why this happened among lemmings, but ultimately concluded, "We may never know."

After several years, the truth about what actually happened started to get out. In 1982, the Canadian Broadcast Corporation aired a documentary called *Cruel Camera* that revealed that the supposed Arctic cliff that the lemmings were jumping off was actually 1,000 miles away from the Arctic Circle. Essentially, the production team had wrangled a couple dozen lemmings from Alaska and shipped them to Calgary. They brought them near the edge of a cliff over the Bow River and set up their cameras. Then the production team started pushing the group of lemmings toward the cliff. When the lemmings nearest the cliff had no more space, the animals fell off. As the humans continued pushing, more and more lemmings appeared to jump. So the Lemming Effect, named after the "mass-follower" suicides by adorable animals, is actually based on the mass cruelty of dozens of animals by humans.

But telling you this awful story isn't just a tangent. It's an example of the Bandwagon Effect. Did you notice it? Members of the production team went along with someone's bad idea and ended up murdering defenseless animals because apparently the rest of the team was okay with a bad idea. Succumbing to the Bandwagon Effect is another error in thinking that can impede our judgments and decisions.

Literally

One bandwagon that many Millennials are jumping on is causing a lot of people frustration—the word "literally" as in, "She *literally* died." Or "He *literally* flew off the handle." Or "His body was *literally* worn to the bone." Why do those phrases cause us so much frustration? Well, it's because they're not using the word correctly! The word comes from the Latin "litera" meaning "letter." The word "literally" is defined by the *Oxford English Dictionary* as "in a literal manner or sense; exactly." Whenever you hear it used incorrectly do you think, "How could you possibly? (You idiot)"

Well, did you know that there is a second definition of the word "literally" in the *Oxford English Dictionary*? The second definition is "used for emphasis, while not being true." Mind your Illusion of Certainty right now. Many of the common responses to this information are, "That can't be correct!" or "That must be a new definition that they added because of the Millennials." Well, that third "Millennial" phrase, "His body was *literally* worn to the bone" was not written by a Millennial. In fact it was written by someone who doesn't belong to any of the generations currently alive. It was written by Charles Dickens in 1839. Since the beginning of the word "literally," it has been used both as an exact representation of things and as a figurative punctuation. Keep in mind how rapidly frustration can consume you when someone sees the world differently than you do, especially if that person is a Millennial. (Full disclosure: I was born on the cusp of the transition from GenX to Millennial, a micro-generation some now refer to as "Xennials." As a "Xennial" with a toe in both GenX and Millennial generations, I have granted myself the authority to both make fun of Millennials and relate to them.)

Along with tribal association, the Bandwagon Effect explains why people group together and pass judgment on a person, a place, or another group of people. The Bandwagon Effect explains how we ended up with thousands of articles written about Millennials, generalizing negative characteristics to an entire generation. If I prompt you by saying, "Millennials are . . . ," what words pop into your mind? I'm betting "lazy," "narcissistic," or "entitled" would be some of the first words you'd imagine. If so, you're like a lot of people. Here's the thing: if we replace the word "Millennials" with any other broad grouping of people, we end up with some really nasty phrases: "Black people are lazy." "Women are narcissistic." "Christians are entitled." All these phrases should ring some moral alarms for us. Most people understand that categorizing an entire group of human beings is both irresponsible and fraught with error. Most of us understand that not all people of a category are exactly the same. We can see that, sure, some men might be narcissistic, but obviously, not all of them. Similarly, some Millennials might feel entitled, but surely, not all of them. Organizations are spending millions of dollars learning how to manage the oncoming Millennial workforce. If only they knew the truth about Millennials.

The Truth about Millennials

What year were the first Millennials born? Interestingly, nobody can agree on when Millennials first arrived on this planet, but there seems to be consensus on what Millennials are like. What we're seeing with the term "Millennials" is tribalism. Neil Howe and William Strouse first coined the term in 1989, when they were thirty-six and forty-years-old. They invented the term as a way to categorize students who would be graduating from high school in the new Millennium. Over time, several additional labels also emerged: "Gen Y," "Generation Next," "Columbine Generation," "9/11 Generation," etc. But none of the labels stuck like "Millennial." With a label like that, people outside that generation could easily identify them as a "they" or an "outgroup." Folks in generations different from Millennials could identify a common enemy, which explains why most of the common assumptions about Millennials are negative. Looking through back issues of magazines, you'll see similar negative assumptions about "Gen X," "Baby Boomers," and the "Greatest Generation." Each new wave comes of age in a slightly different world from the previous generation. Their context and their experiences differ, so each generation understandably has different sets of values and expectations for the world around them.

If you were to identify the first Millennial, you couldn't do it. You also would not be able to state the starting date of the Millennial generation. So-called experts disagree on the official boundaries of the Millennial generation. The starting range is 1977-1985 and the ending range is 1993-2004. But if you define a generation as starting at, say, January 1, 1980, and then attribute traits allegedly unique to that generation, would you say that a person born on that date is different from a person born on December 31, 1979? No, because that starts to sound like astrology. I'm not disparaging astrology, but—well, I suppose I am a little. Being born between April 20 and May 21 does not mean that you are stubborn. Similarly, being born in the 1980s does not make you selfish. We must take into account the infinite variability of humanity. Yes, some people who are born in the 1980s are selfish, but conversely some are generous. It is illogical and irresponsible to place a judgment on nearly two billion people because they were born in a similar time span. United Nations Population Division data indicates that one third of the world population were born in the supposed Millennial start and end years of 1981 and 1997.[21] Even if we narrow our scope and just look at the United States, there are over seventy-five million Millennials. It doesn't make sense to judge all of those people as all having the same personality traits or character flaws. But we seem to do it anyway. When we do this, all we're doing is establishing that they are not in our tribe.

Remember Mike on the family vacations in Phoenix and in Spain? He experienced others and categorized them both outside and inside of his perceived tribe. In Phoenix, when the context made it easy to perceive a Minnesotan accent as "not from around here," the man was not in Mike's tribe and had no authority to suggest a Mexican restaurant. In Spain, however, the context made it easy for Mike to perceive an American accent. Mike felt that the man was part of his tribe. Tribal boundaries are based in perception. They are not fixed, but rather fluid. Remember perception does not equal reality. We are the ones who create these artificial tribal boundaries, and therefore, we have the ability to recreate and redefine them. If you find that you are not relating with someone because they are of a different generation, gender, social class, or country of origin from you, look to find ways in which you are of the same tribe. They are there.

Do You Wanna Race?

As an undergraduate student at Arizona State University, I was required to take a certain number of humanities credits, so I took a course in anthropology. In that class, I was introduced to a mind-blowing concept that shook my understanding about the human experience. My professor shared with us that anthropologists, who study the biological and psychological condition of human societies, have found no biological or genetic markers for distinguishing the race of human beings. In other words, the boundaries of race that we create by using words such as "black" and "white" to describe a person's "race" are not based in biology or a person's DNA. They're based on perceived tribal barriers to identify categories of people. These tribal barriers have been around so long, we have developed a social construct that these perceptions are, in fact reality. They are not.

At that moment, I think most of us in class thought that our professor was clearly an idiot. One person spoke up, "Um, what about skin, eye, and hair color? Those can all be identified in DNA" Then the professor showed us pictures of three men—all with dark brown skin, brown eyes, and black curly hair—and asked us to identify the race of the men. After a brief pause, someone tentatively said, "African-American." The professor acknowledged the student's bravery for speaking up, and then she told the student he was absolutely wrong. In fact, none of the people pictured were American at all. One was from France, one from Russia, and one from South Africa. The takeaway is that the distinctions that we call "race" are not concrete or based in reality. They are tribal boundaries that have been accepted as true. When you realize that the concept of "race" is based in perception and social context rather than some natural reality and then think about the historical results of racial division, you can see how powerfully influential perceived tribal boundaries can be.

Just as race does not have a concrete basis in reality, neither do other common tribal divisions that we use as a framework for our understanding of the world. Think about college rivals. Yes, two people went to different schools; yes, those two schools play each other in sports; but the idea that "they" are the enemy comes from a swift trip up the Perception Escalator. Think about departments like Information Technology (IT) Support and Accounts Payable (AP). One department uses (and breaks) a lot of critical financial software, and the other department fixes all problems relating to computers around the entire organization. When Kathy from AP has an emergent computer issue that is going to prevent checks being cut for vendors, she skirts the typical work ticket process and calls Jennifer, the IT support person directly. Jennifer gets frustrated because "People have no idea what's on my plate, and they think that solving their issue should be my most important task. AP is the worst!"

As soon as Jennifer talks about "they" or "those people," she is reacting to perceived tribal boundaries between herself and AP. She is not reacting to a real division between her and AP, but rather she is using the tribal boundary to create a distinction between who is a part of her group, and who is not.

Schadenfreude

Remember the example from the freeway, when a car zoomed past us driving well above the speed limit and cut us off? We gave them a one-finger salute and grumbled to ourselves about how horrible they were. Let's say we kept driving and five miles down the road, we saw the same car pulled over by a police officer with blue and red lights flashing. What would you feel then? What would you think?

Well, if you're like me or most people, you'd say something like, "Ha! Serves you right!" It feels good to watch the police pull that impatient, arrogant driver over—it might even give you a bit of genuine joy. Many of us have experienced this same feeling when we watch our rival team miss a game-winning shot or when the person who beat us out for a promotion struggles to motivate her team. This is a principle that I call "The Insidious

Nature of Joy from Pain" when we actually experience glee over the misfortune of certain others. I base this principle on the psychological phenomenon called "Schadenfreude." The American Psychological Association breaks down the German words "Shaden," meaning "harm" and "Freude," meaning "joy," to describe how in certain situations, we actually derive joy when certain others are harmed. In some cases, we actually hope for the negative outcomes. There are several examples of The Insidious Nature of Joy from Pain at work, especially after someone we do not respect achieves some success. Have you ever been up for a promotion or applied internally for a new position, and then somehow found out the identity of two of the other candidates you were competing against? The situation is bad, but it's worse if you know one or both of the people personally. Let's say that, for whatever reason, even though you thought that you were the stronger candidate and a better leader, one of these people beat you out and got the job. She's the one who gets to manage a team of twelve people. She's the one who gets to sit in on the manager meetings. She's the one who gets her own office with a window.

After a few months, you start to hear things about her team. You start to hear that people are upset at their new boss. You start to hear that two people have already given notice to leave the organization. All of the chatter around the office is that the team is lacking leadership— leadership that you know you could have provided, if only they had chosen you. You feel a sense of righteous indignation. "Ha! I told you!" You may even feel a bit of joy. That feeling is Joy from Pain. Whether it's because we don't believe the other person deserves it or because we think we deserve more recognition doesn't matter. This feeling comes from the underlying principle that we are separate from the person who beat us out and separate from those who "foolishly" chose someone else over us. We temporarily ignore that the prosperity of the organization as a whole is a common goal.

Consider the Insidious Nature of Joy from Pain outside of the context of work or professional competition. Imagine being out for a jog one summer morning along the beautiful waterfront of Ruston Way in Tacoma,

Washington. Someone passes you on the left because they're a little bit faster. Then a few feet ahead, he trips and breaks his toe and skins his knee. Would you celebrate that misfortune? Of course not. (Well, if you said yes, I think you need a different book.) Our humanity kicks in, and we ask the man if he needs help. Yet many times at work, or on the freeway, or in organized sports, we actively wish for the misfortune of others.

When you pair The Insidious Nature of Joy from Pain with the understanding of tribalism, it can help explain our divisive political climate. Two major political parties have leaned away from center and are beginning to wish misfortune on the other side. When one gains power, it waits for and celebrates failure on the part of the other. We have begun to villainize or demonize members of the opposing party, as if members of the other party were a rival team. We have begun to associate new ideas with either Our Team or Their Team, and if an idea is associated with Their Team, we automatically oppose it, searching for the flaws in logic. We have begun to draw our opinions by echoing the sentiments of prominent members of our team. We have begun to place labels and call "them" names.

When you understand the Joy from Pain, Tribalism, Fight for Right, FAE and the other Principles of Human Understanding I have explained so far, you can see why irrational thoughts and behavior come naturally for human beings. Now that you are aware of these principles at work in yourself and those around you as human beings, what are *you* going to do about it?

What's in a Name?

This is going to sound a little infantile for a few moments, so please bear with me. Do you remember the "name game" that we used to play with our stuffed animals? We would call our giraffe "George the Giraffe" and our Tiger, "Tommy the Tiger." That simple naming convention carries through to some of the characters in children's shows: Bob the Builder, Dora the

Explora (okay, it's Explorer, but we all pronounce it "explora" to rhyme with "Dora").

In their 2002 research, Pelham, Mirenberg, and Jones propose the hypothesis that people have a desire to feel good about themselves, and then they behave according to that desire. They call the phenomenon "Implicit Egotism." Their research indicates that people will choose their profession, physical location, or even mate based on their name. They found that people with last names like Cali, Calin, and Calixto which are relatively rare in the United States (occurring fewer than once per 100,000 people), live in significantly higher frequency in California than anywhere else in the country. People with last names like Penn, Penney, and Pennell live in much higher frequency in Pennsylvania. Why does this happen? What's in a name?

What is your favorite word? Is there a word that you love above all other words? A word that sounds so wonderful to your ears that when it enters your ears for the first time after a few days of absence, it brings a smile to your face? A word that makes your ears perk up and commands your attention, even if you're in the middle of binge-watching your favorite 1990s sitcom on Netflix? A word that Dale Carnegie says is "the sweetest sound in any language"? You got it: your name.

Most of us have a positive association with ourselves, even if we're pessimistic. In fact, that's one of the reasons we make so many of the mistakes described in this book (Illusion of Certainty, Perception / Reality, etc.) We want to present ourselves in the best light. Our image of ourselves is positive, so when we see things and unconsciously relate them to ourselves, we want to see them in the best light, too. We have stronger affinity for those things that we can connect to ourselves. This is why there are so many custom license plate keychains in the bottoms of junk drawers all around the country, or why so many hardware stores are opened by guys named Henry, Harrold, or Harry. This explains why there are so many dentists named Denise, Dena, Dennis, and Denny, and lawyers named Laura, Lauren, Laurie, Lawrence, Larry, and Lance.[22]

The phenomenon of Implicit Egotism is that we are unconsciously egotistical about things that we relate to ourselves, like our name, hometown, alma mater, and birth date. When people feel this connection with someone or something, they unconsciously hope for its goodness or success. Imagine you were on a hiring panel with your boss and a few other people. Your boss, the official hiring manager, ended up hiring John over David, even though you and the other panelists preferred David. The interview process was not out of the ordinary, but it was noteworthy.

A few minutes before John walked into the conference room for his interview, you and the rest of the group was talking about the previous candidate, David, and how wonderful a fit he would be with the energy of the current team. His out-of-the box, yet respectful style would push the team forward in unique ways. Then someone passes out the résumé for the next candidate, John Wheeler. The room falls silent as folks reread John's résumé. A few scratching sounds fill the silence as people begin to scribble notes in the margins of John's résumé, probably trying to cue themselves for the questions they'll want to ask. The conference room door opens, and Neil the receptionist escorts John to the hot seat.

The very first question comes from Bob, the HR liaison, who asks about education experience. Before John answers Bob's question, he apologizes as he pulls out a manila folder and distributes copies of a new résumé. "Since I applied for this job a month ago, John tells the panel, "these are updated copies of my résumé. Last week, I earned my master's degree from the University of Washington, but I didn't want to include that on the résumé before I actually graduated."

Nobody even noticed, but as John said, "University of Washington," your boss's eyes darted up as she took a sharp inhale. It turns out, Jane is an alumnus of the University of Washington. #GoDawgs. From that moment on, it seemed that Jane was trying to make the interview work for John, looking at his résumé and asking him to explain things that were highlighted, rather than asking for "examples of a time. . . ."

Because Jane is also a University of Washington Husky, she had a positive association with the school and wanted graduates the school produces to be successful. Whether or not Jane realized it, she unconsciously wanted John to do well in the interview. She wanted John to have the job. Because his alma mater was the same as hers, her Implicit Egotism caused her to make the (apparently wrong) hiring decision.

Now I know what you're thinking—that's illegal. Bob, the HR guy, should have stopped her. But John was perfectly qualified to hold the position. He had all the experience and, along with his new master's degree, he had more education than the minimum job requirements. This sort of thing happens all the time! Implicit Egotism is in play when we discover we share a birthday or find out someone else has the same name. We remember those people and those situations with a smile. The four other people in the room preferred David, but being the senior member on the panel and the ultimate hiring manager, your boss hired John.

After two years, you wonder why John, who is STILL not able to perform, is still employed by the company. Well, what typically happens is that because your boss took a risk and put her stamp on John, she associated his performance and his continued employment with herself and her reputation. The problem is that because of implicit egotism, your boss wants John, the University of Washington Husky, to succeed. She has become unable to see what is actually going on with his performance. She is not able to assess the situation appropriately in order to make the decisions that need to be made.

I'm explaining Implicit Egotism because it's another bias—a systematic error in thinking that can impact our judgments or decisions. We want our tribe to be successful, so we may make decisions that lean in our tribe's direction. In other words, we have a natural human tendency to gravitate toward those who think like us and have the same background. If we recognize this bias conceptually, we will more likely notice when it shows up and adjust our behaviors accordingly. We might also gently alert the people around us when they might be slipping into biased, irrational thinking. For example, during deliberation for the hiring panel, you might say, "Hey Jane, I think John is a solid candidate and could probably do good work for the company. But I'm a little concerned that because both you and John went to the University of

Washington, you see him slightly more favorably than the rest of us do. Can we revisit the merits of both John and David all together?"

The effect of Implicit Egotism is something else you must watch for in other people and in yourself. Your team, the tribe of coworkers that you choose to identify with at any given moment, will usually show up more favorably in your mind than any other tribe. By now, you can better anticipate and recognize when that happens, analyze the stakes, and decide whether the impact of your Implicit Egotism is totally benign and not necessary to change (like your excitement when your favorite football team wins the Super Bowl), or when it's potentially damaging. In that case, when the stakes are higher and more important, you might want to reconsider your thinking and choose different thoughts and behaviors.

Validation of "Truth"

Remember our librarian Stephan from earlier in the chapter? Because of the Availability Heuristic, you started with the image of a woman. Then as I shared more and more details about our librarian, the hair color, the glasses, the clothing, your brain used all those details as evidence to Validate the "Truth" that your image of a woman librarian was correct. Validation of "Truth" is the eleventh Principle of Human Understanding. (I put "Truth" in quotes here because I am talking about perceptions that we believe to be true rather than facts.) The powerful insight is that you weren't necessarily trying to prove that you were right—you actually didn't think that you could have been wrong. Your brain didn't allow you to think that you were making an assumption; you just believed that you were seeing the situation accurately. Then you used each piece of new information to validate that you were, in fact, correct in the assumption that you didn't realize you made. If you're like most people, when I got to the final detail, the name "Stephan," the Illusion of Certainty kicked in and you experienced a period of disbelief because the evidence no longer matched your assumption. Your presumed certainty may have even been that my editors and I made a typographical error.

This experience describes the psychological phenomenon known as "Confirmation Bias," which means we often look for evidence to confirm that which we already believe to be true. So rather than using the scientific method, looking for evidence to disprove our hypothesis, we end up paying more attention to data that supports our ideas. For instance, were you surprised at the outcome of the 2016 US presidential election? Of course you were. Every single news channel and both candidates were surprised. Yes, BOTH candidates were surprised. Although wanting to win and believing that he could win, Donald Trump didn't expect to win. He hadn't even finalized a victory speech until the night of the election.

But why were we all surprised? To be clear, this is not a political commentary on which candidate was better or how Donald Trump won. This is a powerful example of how the Validation of Truth plays out in real life.

Before the election, thousands of news articles were being published each day, but I want to call attention to two specific articles published three days before the election. One came from *Huffington Post,* a notably liberal-leaning online newspaper, and the other from *FiveThirtyEight.com*, a well-known statistical online news resource. The article from *Huffington Post* leaned on widely shared polling data, stating that candidate Trump had less than a 2 percent chance of winning the election. The article from *FiveThirtyEight.com* leaned on heavy statistics and polls of polls, stating that candidate Trump had a greater than 35 percent chance of winning the election. Guess which one of those two stories was shared more times on social media? The *Huffington Post* story, of course. And it wasn't just liberal-minded people who shared the story. This story and the underlying data were shared by all major news outlets, including CNN, Fox News, MSNBC and more. Because the collective belief of the country was that Hillary Clinton was going to win, any news that confirmed that belief was seen more likely as true, and was, therefore, shared more often. As people validated the "Truth," we all saw more evidence that confirmed that which we already believed.

Beyond the news, The Validation of "Truth" affects us every day. Our friend Samantha had a belief that nobody understood or respected her and the rest of the people who work the night-shift. To her, it wasn't a *belief*—it was a *fact*; it was truth because she had ample evidence to prove that her hypothesis was correct. When she saw the sign, which had obviously been placed there by a day-shift person, she thought to herself, "See, yet another example of day-shift people not thinking about or caring about us." The sign became further evidence that her deeply held belief was correct. Rather than looking to explore what else the sign could have meant, Samantha read the sign and Validated her "Truth."

Social Outcast

Did you know that Confirmation Bias is one of the main reasons that Facebook surpassed two billion monthly active users worldwide? After fourteen years, Facebook absolutely obliterated its former competition into unrecognizable obsolescence. Most people remember MySpace, Facebook's most successful former competitor. At its peak in 2008, MySpace had a monthly user base of nearly seventy-six million monthly users, about 3 percent of Facebook's user base. But MySpace isn't the only former social network; there were many, many others. Few folks remember or have even heard of Friendster, Xanga, Ping, Google+, Orkut, Eons, or Diaspora. All of them were serious social networks that Facebook destroyed with its popularity. I want to talk about one reason that Facebook absolutely took over our digital awareness: Confirmation Bias.

Facebook started building algorithms very early on to identify patterns in what its users "like." This step was fairly easy because the now ubiquitous "like" button made it clear which type of content its various users preferred. Then, Facebook started showing them similar content from similar people, similar emotional sentiment, similar photos, similar videos, etc. Facebook understood the psychology of reinforcing that which you already like, so its users would feel stronger affinity to the platform.

According to PEW research, the median number of "friends" or social connections people have on Facebook is 200. If you use Facebook, you know that there is no way that you are seeing posts from 200 people as you scroll through your news feed. Of course not. You're only seeing a curated list produced by Facebook's algorithm. When you watch a video on Facebook, right afterwards, you see a sampling of "other videos you may like." If you add a friend, you see a list of suggested "other people you may know." Leveraging Confirmation Bias, the algorithm understands what you are most likely to enjoy and presents it to you. Understanding this one universal principle of brain science, Facebook was able to create a product that appealed to more humans than any other product in history.

Frequency Illusion

Another ever-present bias that goes hand in hand with the Validation of "Truth" is Frequency Illusion. Frequency Illusion is something we've all experienced at some point in our lives. Let's say it's time for you to buy a new car. You start looking around at what's out there. Someone tells you about this new sporty sedan that you've never heard of. You start doing some online research, and you find that a nearby dealership has the exact model that you're interested in, in your favorite color. You think that it might be the right car for you, or at least, it's worth a look. So you jump in your old broken-down car, head for the dealership to meet your future car face-to-face, and what do you see on the road? It's the sporty sedan. Suddenly, that sedan's everywhere. It's even in the color you like. Look! There are two at the stop light!

We've all had an experience similar to this, because it's one of the tools that our brains use to recognize patterns. It's not as if there are more of this car on the road right after you became interested in it. But now that your brain has some focus and some excitement about it being the right car for you, it's now also more focused on that object, causing you to see that particular car everywhere you look. The car's always been there, but you couldn't see it before.

When people ask me to explain what I do and what I teach, I will often talk about Frequency Illusion. I ask them about their car. One time, a woman told me she drove a "Hyundai Veloster." I had never heard of a Hyundai Veloster, so I was unsure that the Frequency Illusion would hold. I thought, "Clearly, this is a pretend car with a made-up name, and she's just messing with me." But I went forward anyway. I asked her to recall when she bought her Hyundai Veloster and drove it off of the lot. "What did you see on the road, everywhere?" I asked her. She uttered a resounding "Hyundai Velosters! And in the same orange color as mine!" I briefly wiped the worried beads of sweat from my brow and asked her, "Okay. But what the heck is a Hyundai Veloster?" She let me know it was a little three-door hatchback or "lift-back" with a funky curved back window. Of course I Googled it as soon as I had the opportunity.

Now the funny thing is that since that moment, I see Velosters everywhere! In fact, one time I was driving home from a conference on a two-lane road, and for twelve miles I drove behind—you guessed it—a Hyundai Veloster! From that day on, I've seen Hyundai Velosters on the road almost every time I drive. In fact, it got so ridiculous, that for one month, I started keeping a log with photos of every Hyundai Veloster that I saw and could safely take a photo of. You can even find the photo album on my website www.EricMBailey.com/veloster.

You are now aware of the Hyundai Veloster, especially since I've mentioned it twelve times in this book so far. You are now more likely to see them out on the road. You're welcome. Every time you see a Veloster, I want you to think of me. And if you can snap a picture, tag me on social media @ Eric_M_Bailey.

Confirmation Bias and Frequency Illusion are not by themselves dangerous, but combined with the Illusion of Certainty and FAE, our natural tendency is to find evidence that our judgment is accurate, even if it's not. If we believe that someone is a bad driver, then every time he taps the brakes, we give an internal exasperated sigh (or sometimes an external passive aggressive sigh). From the moment we make the judgment that our boss didn't give us a raise because he's unreasonable, we begin looking for additional evidence that we are correct. Every time he pulls us away from our work for a meeting—unreasonable. Every time he asks us to grab something off the printer for him—unreasonable.

I hope you see now how important it is for you to know these biases exist. If you know that they exist, you can take them out of the shadows and process them with your rational reasoning brain rather than your subconscious emotional brain. Only then, can you be intentional about your behaviors going forward.

Principles of Human Understanding

The Observation Trap Principles

Can trap us by influencing the way we observe the world.

1. The Illusion of Certainty
2. Perception is More Important Than Reality
3. The Desire to Fight to Be Right
4. The Power of Distinction
5. Context is the Underlying Fabric by Which We Encounter the World
6. Empathy Changes Your Judgment

The Orientation Trap Principles

Can trap us by augmenting how we orient ourselves in the world.

7. The Truth About Bias
8. Understanding Fundamental Attribution Error (FAE)
9. The Insidious Nature of Joy from Pain
10. The Fluidity of Tribal Boundaries
11. The Validation of Truth

CHAPTER 4

Decisions

"The risk of a wrong decision is preferable
to the terror of indecision."

—Maimonides

A Tale of Two Brains

Most of us believe that we make thoughtful decisions at work and in our personal lives based on analyzing facts, applying reasoning / logic, and arriving at rational judgments. However, because of the way that the human brain works, there is more going on behind the scenes when it comes to decision-making than we want to believe. You see, rational judgments come from a place that I call the "reasoning brain." But there's another part of our brain that I call the "automatic brain," which operates in a much more rapid and automatic fashion—as the name would suggest. In contrast, the reasoning brain works more slowly.

If you've ever been in a loving, committed relationship, answer these two questions: First, did you (or do you still) love this person? Second question: Why?

Go ahead and answer the questions in your head.

If you're like most people, you had an almost instantaneous answer to my first question: "Yes!" But to my second question, you either didn't answer or you had a relatively delayed answer. This phenomenon happens because answering a yes/no question like "Do you love this person?" can be answered by the automatic brain with a "yes" almost instantaneously. But when you try to answer the "Why do you love this person?" question, your brain needs time to give you reasons. This reasoning process happens in the reasoning brain and takes longer. In other words, your delay in identifying reasons doesn't indicate that you don't or didn't actually love that person—it just reflects a slower process in the brain. The automatic brain reacts to your emotions but has no access to the language center, where words are formed. So when I asked the "why" question, the automatic brain is of no use. This two-brain concept helps us understand the Truth About Judgment and Decisions, which is the twelfth Principle of Human Understanding. While we believe that we make judgments and decisions with our reasoning brain, it's important to know that we also make judgments and decisions using our automatic brain.

Let's try an exercise that I call "The Two Capital Facts" exercise. I will list two different facts, one of them false and one of them true. After I list the two facts, you will probably have an idea about which fact is true and which fact is false. After I list the facts, I'll ask some questions. Here we go:

Fact One:

France has twelve time zones.

Fact Two:
The capital of Switzerland is Geneva.

It's clear to me, mainly because I designed this exercise, that the second fact, "The capital of Switzerland is Geneva," is clearly false.

Does that surprise you? In fact, most people who read this will be at least moderately surprised that the second fact is false. Maybe you weren't certain either way, but you had a stronger feeling toward the second fact compared to the first. This feeling did not surface because of the Illusion of Certainty or Availability Heuristic, but rather because our brains are more predictably influenced than we care to believe. Let's dive deeper into this.

That Was Easy

The reason that the first fact seems to be false and the second fact seems to be true is in the way our brain responds to new information, like the possible number of time zones in a relatively small country. As we take in new information, context can make it easier or harder for our brains to receive and process the information. There are certain contextual elements in the two facts that can aid or distract you from receiving and processing the information with something known as "Processing Fluency." According to Alter and Oppenheimer, researchers at NYU and Princeton respectively, Processing Fluency is the experience of how easy it is for your brain to take in new information.[23] For example, when you read information displayed in an easy-to-read font, it's easier for your brain to interpret; therefore, you processed the fact about the capital of Switzerland (written above in a large, clear font) with fluency. Due to the greater fluency, you are more likely to trust or believe the information as true.

Another contextual element for cognitive ease is repetition. You'll notice this in commercial advertisements when you see the same product advertised over and over again. Every time you see some concept, image, or idea repeated, your brain has a hint of recognition and receives that information more easily. The name of the exercise I asked you to perform was the "Two Capital Facts Exercise." In reality, the exercise didn't really match the title that I gave it. The only reason I gave the exercise this title is that the second fact about Switzerland had the word "capital" in it. In other words, I gave the exercise that title purely to repeat the word "capital." And because the word was repeated, your brain received the information about Switzerland's capital with more processing fluency, and therefore, found the second fact easier to believe.

The third contextual clue is color contrast. Just as with the easy-to-read font, it is easier for your brain to perceive what you are looking at when there is more contrast. In fact, your brain finds images with higher contrast more pleasing. This helps explain almost all the automatic photo filters on your phone or on Instagram. They add color tinting and other tricks, but almost all of them add contrast. As you can see, the first fact above is presented with a lighter font color on white paper and with a more difficult-to-read script font. Both elements (font and less contrast) cause cognitive stress, which means it's harder for your brain to interpret the message in the first fact.

Processing fluency is perceived by our automatic brain, our fast-thinking brain. Under most circumstances at work and at home, we like to believe that we are making thoughtful, rational judgments and decisions. But that kind of thinking happens in our slower reasoning brain, so a word of caution: many of the judgments and decisions you make daily are actually influenced by processing fluency and cognitive stress. Therefore, your automatic brain makes quick judgments and decisions based on feelings and emotions before your reasoning brain even has a chance to reason. Then, after a period of time, your reasoning brain kicks in and provides you reasonable explanations for why you made that judgment or decision. What's more, Perception > Reality and the Illusion of Certainty cause you to believe that the reasons you came up with are, in fact, the real reasons you made your judgment or decision. As much as you want to believe that you are in control of your judgments and decision-making through reasoning, logic, and facts, it's important to realize that part of your brain is actively working against you (and consequently against the boss, the company, the coworkers, or the conditions at work that you're judging).

Oh, and by the way, France *does* have twelve time zones. In fact, it has the most time zones of any country on earth. This only makes sense, though, when you remember that France has territories all over the world. And the capital of Switzerland is not Geneva, it's Berne.

Brain Fried

There's something new that's been rolling out slowly across the United States at McDonald's. Have you heard of it? The folks at McDonald's are changing their french fries. Based on nearly five years of focus groups and product testing, McDonald's is switching to larger, wedge-style french fries. They determined that the larger potato wedges require fewer cuts per potato, and therefore, can be made faster than the current thinner fries. Customer feedback was inconclusive, so they determined that the cost savings far outweighed any decline in customer satisfaction. Over the next year, they will be rolling out their new fries across the country. If you would like to see a photo of the new fries, visit my website at www.EricMBailey.com/fries.

Pay attention to the tone of your thoughts right now. Are you having an emotional reaction to this news about McDonald's new fries? Many folks I talk to have an emotional reaction to the change. "They can't do that!" people say. "McDonald's french fries are a part of my history!" Then they start telling stories about their past, just like I did when I first heard about the change. When I was a little child and had to stay home sick, my grandma and grandpa watched me. My mom dropped me off at my grandparent's house early in the morning, and we watched a little TV before grandma had to go to work. My grandfather drove my grandmother to work with me in the back seat. About one mile into the drive, we went through the McDonald's drive-thru. This happened every single time I was sick; it was sort of a ritual. We would go through the drive-thru, and my grandparents would order two coffees, four sugars, four Equals (because my grandfather was diabetic), and four cream packets (my grandparents each needed two creams). I ordered a Happy Meal with chicken nuggets (which always had the same weird shapes) and the french fries. As soon as the Happy Meal box entered the car window, all the air in the car was instantly improved by the aroma of the fries! Those french fries helped define my childhood. So when someone suggested that the french fries were changing, I, like so many others, felt as if a part of my history was being changed without my consent.

Now that, my friends, is the epitome of an emotional, automatic brain response. The rapid reaction that "This is bad! They can't do that!" is the brain's judgment of the presented information. If your slower, reasoning brain processed all the information, you would likely be feeling different right now.

Rest assured, though, this story about McDonald's changing their fries is not true. They are not planning on changing your beloved french fries. If you would have calmed your automatic brain and reasoned your way through, you would have realized that McDonald's would not change their french fry recipe like that. They might add potato wedge "McPatatas," like they have in some South American and European countries, but they're not going to replace their fries.

Even if you didn't have an emotional response to this exercise, just know that many folks who read this fake announcement about McDonald's french fries had an automatic, fast-brain judgment or reaction. Be careful how you respond to people who have emotional reactions to information. Because their emotional response comes from their automatic brain, so, too, can your automatic, fast-brain make an emotional judgment of them. "How could you possibly get worked up over fries?" Remember, I just warned you a few sentences ago that when you believe you're making reasonable, rational judgments and decisions, part of your brain is actively working against you. It's important to understand that this reaction is something that affects all people. When people respond emotionally to some action, understand that their response is not irrational, but rather, a totally normal function of the human brain.

Let's check back in on Karl and Samantha in the break room. As you'll recall, Karl, who is usually the first one in the office in the morning, printed and posted a rather snarky sign to vent his frustration about the coffee pot not being cleaned at the end of the day. Because of his frustration, he created an arbitrary rule that said that the pot needed to be cleaned after 4:00

p.m. He also hinted that anyone who didn't clean the pot was an animal. Samantha, on the other hand, who is usually the last one in the office at night, tore down the sign and was going to throw it away. Who was wrong? Who was right?

You may have assigned a judgment to both of their behaviors and possibly felt emotionally connected to either Samantha or Karl because of some similar experience you identified with. In fact, both employees acted irrationally, and if you understand where their irrational behavior came from, they also both acted logically. Both did things that could be judged as wrong, and both did things that could be judged as right.

When Samantha saw the sign, she processed it through her emotional automatic brain, piling on all her beliefs about how the rest of the office doesn't understand the late-shift folks. Karl's sign further validated the "truth" as she saw it that the rest of the office doesn't care about night-time employees. Reading the sign sent Samantha ascending the Perception Escalator into an immediate spark of rage and anger. She reacted by tearing down the sign just as Karl walked back into the break room.

Similarly, when Karl saw that the sign was gone and realized that Samantha had torn it down and crumpled it up, he, too, became angry. "How could you possibly think it's okay to tear down that sign?" This was more of a statement than a question. There's that phrase again, "How could you possibly...?" And remember this phrase's subtext: "You're an idiot." This time, Samantha heard Karl's subtext loud and clear.

Of course, Karl also judged the situation based on his own experience. He put up the sign because he believed that nobody appreciated him for all the good work he does in the morning for the entire office by coming in early and making coffee. Seeing Samantha tear down the sign validated his "truth" about not being appreciated, just like Samantha felt validated, only for a different reason. Instead of trying to understand the other person's motivation, the two coworkers get into an argument, trying to build stronger and stronger cases for their own position.

"How could you possibly think it's okay to tear down that sign?"

"Oh, was that your sign?" Samantha asks. Then without waiting for Karl's response, she adds, with a healthy dose of sarcasm, "I should have guessed."

Remember, speaking in evolutionary terms, part of Samantha's snarky reaction is in response to being called an "animal." Her body was reacting as if she were being attacked by a Sabre-tooth tiger. Fight or Flight. This time, it was the former.

"What's that supposed to mean?" asks Karl, matching Samantha's attitude.

"You people are always trying to make the rules," says Samantha. "You don't care about anyone else."

We know that when Samantha say, "you people," she means "day-shift" people, but do you think that Karl knows that? No. Karl, who is Latinx, hears a negative judgment about his Latin American heritage, which sends him to another level of rage. At this point in the conversation, the coffee pot no longer matters. Both Samantha and Karl are trying to win, but both are standing on incomplete information to do so. They are only listening enough to be offended or exasperated by what the other person is saying, just waiting for the moment to insert their next point in to the conversation. Both coworkers' emotions are running high and their voices are getting louder as a crowd begins to form in the break room.

The OODA Loop

Let's pause for a moment to understand what's happening between Karl and Samantha by learning about "the OODA Loop" (pronounced as a word, not as a series of letters). In 2018, I was inducted as an Honorary Commander in the 63rd Fighter Squadron at Luke Air Force Base. The following example of the OODA Loop was vetted for accuracy by three amazing fighter pilots, Brigadier General Brook "Tank" Leonard, Lieutenant Colonel Curtis "Cooter" Daughtery, and Lieutenant Colonel Dave "Fuge" Francis.

You are a fighter pilot in a scenario that's just like every dogfight scene in the movies. You're flying along, and all of a sudden, you think you see incoming aircraft on the horizon. Your flight briefing didn't include information that anyone would be flying in that area, so you don't expect anyone else from your squadron, nor do you hear anything on the radio. What do you do? Do you run? Do you turn? Do you jettison weapons so you're more agile for a fight? What you need to do is put yourself in the OODA loop.

In a 1996 briefing entitled, *The Essence of Winning and Losing*,[24] Colonel John Boyd of the US Air Force explains the OODA loop, the method that fighter pilots use to make rapid decisions in a rapidly changing environment. OODA stands for Observe, Orient, Decide, Act. And it's a loop because just like the Perception Escalator, your actions and the other pilot's actions or reactions change the environment and start the process over and over again. For example, if you were flying at 690 miles per hour (1,126.5 kph) and an unknown incoming aircraft suddenly appeared on the horizon, you would need to make a decision and act. Since the incoming aircraft is flying toward you head on, the relative speed is over 1,300 miles per hour (2,000 kph). Additionally, your perspective will change along the way (traveling at nearly a quarter mile per second tends to do that). After you act, you need to re-Observe the situation, Re-Orient yourself, Decide what to do, and Act again. And then the loop starts over again.

I was introduced to the OODA loop in 2013 by Josh Schneider and George Mitnacht, a pair of former Recon Marines, two of the finest gentlemen and most effective leaders I have ever had the opportunity to work with. They ran the project management department at a rapidly growing healthcare firm that desperately needed project management. They taught me to see that when people are stuck in a certain way of thinking (or stuck in erroneous thinking that they know the solution to a problem), they fail to re-orient to the current circumstances, and therefore, they cannot make proper decisions. In project management, or in all management for that matter, people need to constantly make decisions that have measurable impact on the situation and the surrounding environment. If you fail to take into account the changes in the environment, you miss important information for future decisions.

Here's an example. At 6:00 p.m. on Sunday, March 31, 2019, the Blockbuster Video store in Morley Australia closed its doors for the last time, leaving the store in Bend, Oregon as the only remaining Blockbuster Video store left in the world. While it's still a functional video rental store, it's also become a photo opportunity for nostalgic tourists who remember how popular Blockbuster used to be. If you don't remember, Blockbuster was the world's largest video rental company, with over 9,000 locations around the world at its peak in 2004. For many people, going to Blockbuster on a Friday evening was the starting point for movie night and a wonderful weekend. But the company's failure to navigate the OODA Loop caused poor decision-making and had a measurable impact on outcomes.

Right in the middle of Blockbuster Video's growth in the late 1990s and early 2000s, Netflix, a small startup video delivery company started to flounder. Incorporated in 1997, this innovative service tried to compete with Blockbuster by moving the selection and rental process online, then packaging Digital Video Discs (DVDs) into envelopes and mailing them out to customers to keep for as long as customers wanted them. The Netflix approach to video rental was visionary, but they were not managed very well. In the year 2000, Reed Hastings, the founder of Netflix, approached the CEO of Blockbuster and offered to sell the company for $50 million. At the time, even though Netflix had over 300,000 monthly paying subscribers, they were heavily reliant on the expensive United States Postal Service. The sale proposal was for Netflix.com to change its name to "Blockbuster.com" and handle the forthcoming online side of movie rentals. Blockbuster, in turn, would handle the in-store rentals. Blockbuster's CEO, John Antioco, turned down the deal. Barry McCarthy, the Chief Finance Officer for Netflix at the time, remembers the meeting with Antioco. In a 2008 podcast interview with The Unofficial Stanford Blog, McCarthy recalls, "They just about laughed us out of their office. They thought that we were a small niche business."[25] Antioco couldn't have been more wrong.

At one point, Netflix was listed on the NASDAQ as worth over $150 billion (3,000 times the offer price!). By recounting Blockbuster's fate, I am not saying that the former CEO of Blockbuster was not a visionary; that is not my point. At the first opportunity to purchase Netflix, Antioco may have properly observed the business environment and made the right decision. My point is that he failed to orient and observe as the world changed around him. He didn't properly use the OODA loop: Observe, Orient, Decide, Act. Observe, Orient, Decide, Act. If he had, he might have missed the $50 million offer, but a year later, he could have tried for a $100 million offer. The impact of the Blockbuster CEO's decision not to purchase Netflix is ultimately the reason that many tourists visit Bend, Oregon each year . . . to take a selfie in front of the one remaining Blockbuster video store.

In the break room, Karl and Samantha were both Deciding and Acting (reacting), but they were both missing Observation and Orientation. In their escalating argument, they failed to recognize a growing body of contextual cues—the growing crowd, the other person's elevating volume and intensity—that would have alerted them that they were on the wrong path. If Samantha were to properly go through the OODA Loop, she could have caught herself at multiple opportunities and changed her decisions. As she pulled down the sign and saw Karl walk in getting upset, she could have Observed that he was reacting to his sign being torn down. She could have Oriented to that and realized that it was not entirely necessary to do that. She could have Decided that, even though she wanted to tell Karl something, she should apologize for tearing down the sign, and then Acted by apologizing. Imagine how the entire conversation would have turned out if it had started with an apology. Imagine how Karl would have received Samantha's concerns and frustrations if he had started by Observing a genuine apology and reOrienting to a place of forgiveness.

Just OODA It!

Skipping parts of the OODA Loop leads to poor decisions, but so, too, does getting stalled, which is the thirteenth Principle of Human Understanding.

Just as we find ways to get stuck on steps of the Perception Escalator, we can get stuck on certain parts of the OODA Loop. Whether or not you are a fighter pilot, you are constantly at some point in the OODA loop as you encounter the world around you. At work, when you walk into the break room and find that people are gossiping, OODA. When you believe that you've given clear instructions and someone fails to meet your expectations, OODA. Or when you're online and someone posts something critical or offensive to you, OODA. Unfortunately, far too often, we're stuck at the D (Decide) or at the A (Act), and we fail to make a decision, or we fail to act. Or we fail to properly orient ourselves to the situation, causing inaccurate observations, flawed decisions, and wrong actions.

Think about a big decision you're currently facing, whether at work or at home. What is keeping you from making the decision and Acting? Do you feel that you don't have enough information? Or is it something more basic? Often, we are mired in indecision because we have some fear about the outcome. But if we properly orient ourselves to the situation and to the context, we can make accurate observations. Based on those observations, we can make a decision.

Matt is one of those people at work that spends (wastes) a lot of time complaining. He complains about his boss, he complains about his co-workers, he complains about meetings, he complains about his work load, he complains just about everything. You've probably had this thought just after talking to a person like Matt: "Well, if you hate it so much, why don't you do something about it?"

The reason that Matt won't change his job or talk to his boss or his co-workers is that he is stuck in the Decide and Act phases of the Loop. Being stuck at one part of the OODA Loop can be just as detrimental to achieving desired outcomes as skipping parts. Many of us have an experience where we want to do something, or we say that we want to do something, but don't actually take the step to accomplish it. We're stuck. We want to lose weight, we want to gain muscle, we want to start a project, we want to finish a project, we want to start a business, we want to save more money, we want to make more money, we want to volunteer more, we want to stop wasting so much time on social media, we want to get to know our employees better, we want to wake up earlier, we want to read more. But we don't because we're stuck. Just OODA it!

Here's another example. I grew up with a guy who wanted to write a nonfiction book. He read voraciously and loved how the best authors (Ken Blanchard, Jim Collins, Malcolm Gladwell, John Kotter, Daniel Pink, Brené Brown, and others) could cause him to think differently about the world around him. He also read many other books that were either too academic (and boring), or too entertaining (and intellectually thin). For well over a decade, he had grand ideas of writing his own book, but never did it. In other words, he made it through the Observe and Orient phases of the OODA Loop, but he got stuck in fear before he finally Decided and Acted. He *declared* that he made the decision to write the book, but he never made a true Decision.

Author and international life-changer Tony Robbins wrote in his 2012 book *Awaken the Giant Within*, "A real decision is measured by the fact that you've taken a new action. If there's no action, you haven't truly decided."[26] Once our want-to-be author cleared that Decision step (with the help of key family members, friends, and business colleagues), he took Action and spent the next year waking up at six o'clock in the morning writing his book one hour at a time before his family woke up. He wrote a book that is changing *your* life at this very moment! In short, I just OODA'd it!

Mostly, the fear we experience about taking action (applying for that new position, starting your business, or moving across the country) is because we're not sure (or not assured) about the outcome. Our brain fears the unknown: *What if I'm not capable of performing well in that new position? What if I'm not successful? What if I hate living and working in Boston?* In her leadership workshop, "Nine Strategies for Relentlessly Pursuing Personal and Professional Success," my friend and business partner, Nicole Lance poetically declares, "The fear is greater than the fallout!"

If you think about it, when there's something you've never done before, there's no way you'll know with absolute certainty what the outcome will be *unless* you do it. The Illusion of Certainty will make you believe that you know, but you can't know because it hasn't happened. You can make an educated guess that may turn out to be right, but you don't *know*. Remember, the only things in life that you can learn are things that you don't yet know. If you look back over the course of your life, you'll see a string of decisions that can be judged one of two ways, good or bad. I'm willing to bet that in exactly 100 percent of those decisions, good or bad, you survived. And I'm fairly certain of that because you're reading this book! If you remember that OODA is a loop, even when you make a "wrong" decision, you have the opportunity to reorient and ultimately make another decision.

As human beings, we often let fear stop us because we believe that the ultimate result of the fear is the final state. Our brains would have us believe that we're going to have to live in that final state forever. But that isn't the case. Now, I'm not saying that our actions don't have lasting consequences; they do. But consequences are not final. Consequences become the new environment in which we must Observe and Orient to. We will make more decisions and actions in the future, each of them slightly changing our environment. After every "wrong" decision or misstep you've made in life to this point, you've followed up with subsequent decisions. Even the bad outcomes were not permanent—they were just followed by other outcomes.

So if you've been stuck in your OODA loop on a particular decision, jump on out there and take action. Remember, no matter what decision you make and what subsequent action you take, you will also have the opportunity to re-Observe and re-Orient so that you can Act again. Just OODA It!

Principles of Human Understanding

The Observation Trap Principles

Can trap us by influencing the way we observe the world.

1. The Illusion of Certainty
2. Perception is More Important Than Reality
3. The Desire to Fight to Be Right
4. The Power of Distinction
5. Context is the Underlying Fabric by Which We Encounter the World
6. Empathy Changes Your Judgment

The Orientation Trap Principles

Can trap us by augmenting how we orient ourselves in the world.

7. The Truth About Bias
8. Understanding Fundamental Attribution Error (FAE)
9. The Insidious Nature of Joy from Pain
10. The Fluidity of Tribal Boundaries
11. The Validation of Truth

The Decision Trap Principles

Can trap us by leading us to make uninformed decisions.

12. The Truth About Judgment / Decisions
13. Just OODA It!

CHAPTER 5

Destruction from Distraction

"The age in which we live, this non-stop distraction,
is making it more impossible for the young generation
to ever have curiosity or discipline."

–Vivenne Westwood, Fashion Designer

Squirrel!

Do you remember the talking dog named Doug from the Disney movie, *UP*? He had a device around his neck that turned his barking vocalizations into English words. Doug would be having a wonderful conversation with the main characters and then, without warning, right in the middle of a sentence, he would jerk his head to the right and shout, "SQUIRREL!" This idea of the squirrel, or "shiny object" that can instantly and inappropriately consume our attention, illustrates how quickly and completely we can become distracted from the task at hand. In *UP*, distractedness gets exaggerated, but the experience of losing focus happens to us all the time at work ("Did I remember to email Jamie my TPS report?")

When you're supremely focused on the task at hand, all it takes to become distracted is for you to think about the sound a Coca-Cola makes when it's poured over crystal clear ice cubes in a frosted, perspiring glass in a commercial. You hear the familiar clinking sound of the ice cubes tapping the sides of the glass as the cool liquid lifts them up. As you watch those tiny carbonation bubbles popping out the top, you're anticipating the familiar sound of perfect sensory satisfaction, "Ahhhhhhhhhhhhhhhhhhhhhhhhhhhh." The Fundamental Attribution Error becomes little more than a missed line of information. As much as you want to stay focused on reading that file, you can't get the image of that Coke out of your head. In fact, you'll likely have to reread the previous sentence to realize it was complete gibberish.

So what's going on? Your visual and auditory memory of a commercial with a Coke being poured lights up the parts of your brain that would light up if you were actually experiencing the Coke being poured. As your attention was focused on the Coke, it's much harder to take in new information. While you're still able to read the words on the page, you typically switch your brain to auto pilot and the words you're reading don't actually get processed or comprehended. They don't stick. If you've ever read a high school or college level textbook, you understand what I'm talking about. Sometimes your mind wanders, and you have to re-read a paragraph several times because it's so boring, you don't actually process the information. (Wait, I think I just planted the seed in your mind that this book might be boring . . . Moving on!)

The point here is distraction can have a detrimental effect on your cognitive abilities.

Get Smart

One distraction we deal with on an almost constant basis is from our so-called "connected devices." We are told that these devices are connected to people, the world, and just about everything. But the reality is that these devices are connected to the internet. While it's true that we can use these devices to have conversations or interactions with people across large expanses of space and time, frequently, we use these devices as a shield from having real contact with real humans right in front of us.

We have all witnessed a group having dinner together at a restaurant.

But every person at the table is looking down at his or her device, rather than talking, listening to, or laughing with each other. We've also all had the experience of standing in a group of people, and when one person draws out their device to check some notification, what does everyone else do? One-by-one, they all pull out their own devices to check their own notifications. It's almost as if we're afraid to be the one person not on our device. We check notifications out of fear that we've missed something important—or we fear we might be bored!

Watching this scenario play out dozens of times a day, it seems as if we're losing the ability to just be present with others and present with our own thoughts. This change is meaningful because research indicates that creativity happens in the space of solitude. In her book *Quiet: The Power of Introverts in a World That Won't Stop Talking*, author Susan Cain posits that many artists, actors, directors, musicians, and other "creative" professionals are introverts. Even though there is no official psychological definition of the term "introvert," the term is commonly understood to refer to people who prefer to gain energy and process their thoughts in solitude. Extroverts, on the other hand, tend to gain energy and process their thoughts among other people. Oversimplified, introverts think and then speak; extroverts speak as they think.

If you didn't know, introverts make up about half the population, so chances are, if you're not an introvert, there's one near you. To be clear, introversion is not the same thing as shyness. Introverts can be shy, but so can extroverts. Cain explains, "Shyness is the fear of social disapproval or humiliation, while introversion is a preference for environments that are not overstimulating. Shyness is inherently painful; introversion is not."[27] Encountering an introvert at work or in a personal situation can baffle an extrovert—and vice versa. Each of us often finds it difficult to understand people who see the world differently from the way we do. We even start saying things like, "How could you possibly. . . ."

Imagine, for example, that you're leading a project team of twelve people. At the beginning of the project, you want to surface and organize as many ideas as possible. Then you plan to group the ideas into categories for your team to begin exploring. After gathering your entire team into the conference room, everyone has a seat around the table except for you. You're standing with a marker at the whiteboard ready to record ideas. After introducing the meeting, you say, "Alright, let's do some brainstorming. What ideas do you think could make us wildly successful? Ready, GO!"

Crickets.

Eventually one brave person throws out an idea that's not revolutionary, but it isn't totally bland either. You write it down and offer some praise. Then you urge the group to "keep 'em coming." At the end of your thirty-minute meeting, you've filled the whiteboard and feel like you've really democratized the creative process. The problem? You likely haven't.

Guess what? When you thrust people into a brainstorming session, or what I like to call, "an extrovert's playground," you're actually hampering the creative process. Many of us have been taught since grade school that brainstorming is the best way to collaborate and surface a lot of creative ideas out. But if creativity happens in solitude, the very act of typical brainstorming can have the opposite effect. If you also understand that introverts like to think before they speak, it's less likely that they will offer off-the-cuff ideas in a brainstorming session. So theoretically, you could be leaving your meeting with a whiteboard filled with ideas that came from only about half your team.

Now fortunately, you can make a couple of easy adjustments to fix brainstorming that will improve the creative flow and volume of ideas. First, you should let people know in advance that you're holding a brainstorming session. Also, if it's appropriate let them know the questions you intend to answer or problems you intend to solve. This way the breadth of the brainstorm isn't overwhelming. Second, ask people to walk into the meeting with a few creative ideas (I typically suggest three to five) to solve the problem or answer the question. These two modifications to brainstorming allow for creativity in solitude before sharing ideas out loud. The method enables introverts to think first and then speak. You'll likely find greater participation from both introverts and extroverts, and you might walk away with more (and better) ideas on the whiteboard.

If we are creating a society in which we are railing against the perceived agony of solitude and boredom—almost constantly surrounding ourselves with stimuli—what do you believe the impact will be on our creativity? If we use our "connected" devices to protect ourselves from being bored or being present with other people, we're losing the capacity to be creative and collaborate. We use our "connected devices" to do an infinite number of tasks and activities, constantly ensuring that we are not bored in solitude. Paradoxically, the developers that create applications for these devices typically work in solitude as they develop them. What could we create if we allowed ourselves a little more solitude?

"Yes, yes, Eric, I understand that creativity happens in solitude. But what should I do about it? Should I add it to the list of things that I 'should' do, but I just don't have time for?"

The issue of time comes up with nearly every one of my client partners. Both bosses and employees say that they wish they had more resources to accomplish their goals. They say that they need more time, money, or staff. I frequently hear people say, "If I only had the budget, I'd be able to tackle my strategic priorities." Or, "If I only had a few extra hours in every week, I'd be more effective." But we've been saying things like this our entire careers. Here's an example: If you think back to when you got your first job, let's say you were sixteen years old, how much money did you make? And how much did you want to make? For me, I was a busser at the Outback Steakhouse making $4.80 per hour. When I got my first paycheck, my eyes opened wide. All of a sudden, I could see the future. All of a sudden, I had earned my own money and was a contributing member of society. After my third paycheck, I started doing the math on how much MORE money I could make if I worked more hours. After my fifth paycheck, I realized that more hours is nice, "but if I made $10 per hour, I would be set for life!" The resources that our teenage selves needed "to be set for life" are likely far below what we are currently making. The amount is so low, it's almost preposterous. And yet, we have repeated the same sentiment over and over across our careers. "If I only had the money, the time, the resources, I would truly be happy."

This type of irrational thinking reflects human beings' ability to slide our expectations along a continuum commensurate with our achievement. As we have more resources, we tend to want more resources. A few months after we achieve $30,000, we begin the transition to wanting $35,000. Psychologists call this phenomenon the "Hedonic Treadmill." The Hedonic Treadmill is the theory that an adjustment to salary (or another resource) temporarily lifts our happiness, but due to adaptation, we quickly get used to the new resource level and our happiness returns to where it was before. It's not the raise or the additional resources that will make us happier, it's how we choose to see them and use them.

We have a fundamental inability to understand the concept of "enough." So, if we had more time, we'd waste more time. According to Parkinson's Law, "work expands to fill the time available for its completion." Sometimes referred to as the "Procrastinator's Law," Parkinson's Law indicates that if a job needs to be done and there are a set number of hours to do it, our natural reaction is to say that we don't have enough time, but we'll still get it done. However, if we were given 20 percent less time to get the job done, we would similarly claim that we didn't have enough time—but we'd still get it done. The resource (time) is not the true constraint. The true constraint is what we choose to do with our resources.

In his wildly popular 2006 TED Talk, Tony Robbins walks into a powerful and potentially emotionally charged exchange with former Vice President Al Gore who was seated in the front row. In a moment of interaction with the audience, Robbins asks the group if they have ever failed to achieve a meaningful project in their lives. As the camera pans the audience, we can see that a vast majority of folks raised their hands. Robbins asks why they didn't achieve success in the project. He prompts them with the phrase, "I didn't have the . . . ." Then audience members can be heard shouting out completions to the sentence. Robbins repeats several of their completion phrases: "I didn't have the knowledge. I didn't have the time. I didn't have the money." Then someone in the front row shouts something inaudible. For a split second, Tony Robbins breaks his professorial affect with an enormous grin. He then repeats what he heard from this audience member: "I didn't have the Supreme Court." As the audience realizes the comment came from Al Gore, they erupt in laughter and applause. Of course, Gore was referencing the highly contested campaign during the presidential election of 2000 when the Supreme Court intervened and ultimately ruled that Gore lost the election to George W. Bush by the slim margin of 271 to 266 Electoral College votes. Robbins was so delighted by Al Gore's participation, that he walked down off the stage and gave Gore a high five.

Once back on the stage, still with a giant smile on his face, Robbins continued his talk, incorporating Gore's stated reason for losing the presidency. "What do all of these things, including the Supreme Court, have in common? They are a claim to you missing resources. And while they may be accurate, they are not the defining factor." Again, the audience erupts in laughter, although this time the crowd's a little rowdier because they realize that Tony Robbins is publicly stating that Al Gore's excuse for losing the election is wrong. The camera pans to Gore in the front row, who can be seen belly laughing in a makes-your-mouth-hurt-from-smiling-so-big laugh. Robbins continues: "The defining factor is never resources. It's resourcefulness." In other words, it's not what you have; it's how you use what you have. When you begin to claim that you don't have enough time, think, instead, "I have as much time as everyone. What am I doing with the time that I have?" I want to repeat this, "I have as much time as everyone. What am I doing with the time that I have?"

When I interview executives, time-based resources are routinely in the top three scarcest resources. My first response is, "What are you doing with your time?" Research studies can answer this question. In 2016, a study from Salary.com asked people to anonymously self-identify how much time they wasted on technology on an average workday. The answers were shocking. Eighty-nine percent of workers stated that they waste at least thirty minutes each workday on technology. About 62 percent of workers waste more than one hour per day on technology. As I've shared that information with groups around the country, I've found that people are often surprised because they believe that these numbers are too low!

At one hour each day, that makes five wasted hours per week on technology. What would you do with five hours extra every week? You could accomplish that project you've been working on. You could really dive into the exercise program that you've been putting off. You could accomplish all your home project list in a couple of weeks. Or, as crazy as it sounds, with an extra five hours per week, you could leave work on time every day. Imagine what's possible when you properly use your resources. Imagine what's possible when you let go of your connected devices and temporarily loosen their grip on your attention.

A study from the University of Texas Austin found that the mere presence of cell phones on our desks makes us dumber. Well, they didn't use the word "dumber"; they said, "the mere presence of cell phones reduces our cognitive ability,"[28] but you know what I'm talking about. The researchers explain that there are two reasons this happens. First, it takes effort for us to avoid looking at our phone when it's on the desk or table next to us. If we're trying to have a conversation with somebody or trying to accomplish a task, it takes actual effort for us not to look at our phone. (As I was writing that last sentence, I literally grabbed my phone off the desk for no reason. After chuckling at the irony, I hid it from myself under a folder.) As our devices sit there in plain view on our desks, even face down, we have to actively try not to look at them. That effort uses some of our cognitive capability, leaving fewer cognitive resources available for the task or conversation at hand.

The second reason researchers offered for why phones make us dumber is that when we glance at our phones, our brains switch tasks to all the things we could be doing with our phones: checking notifications, emails, our video doorbell, Facebook, playing games, and the endless other activities we use our phones for. Even if we're not doing these tasks when we glance at our phone, our brain temporarily switches to all those tasks we could be doing. As we restore our attention to the task or conversation at hand, our brain switches back. This task switching is rapid, but not instantaneous—it takes a period of time for us to ramp back up to the level of focus and attention that we had before.

To illustrate what I mean by "ramping back up," think about the last time you entered a room and completely forgot the purpose of walking in the room in the first place. Eventually you figured it out, but this experience is the same process your brain goes through when it switches away from a task and switches back. If you would like to experience this cognitive depletion in a fun way, visit my website at www.EricMBailey.com/brain and look for "Destruction from Distraction." This will lead you to an exercise there called the Stroop Test. In the exercise, I show you a series of shapes. Your job is to simply identify the color of the shapes. In doing this, several simple distractions are introduced. Because of the distractions, the typical adult will find it increasingly difficult to accomplish the task. Some will stop trying altogether. You will experience the actual cognitive decline caused by distraction. The Cognitive Destruction from Distraction is the fourteenth Principle of Human understanding. Whether it's from technology, stress, or competing priorities, we are not at our best when we are distracted.

Technology is so ubiquitously integrated into our regular daily habits that we don't even see them as distractions anymore. It's now possible for iPhones and Android phones to track how much time you're spending on certain applications and alert you if you're spending too much time on your phone or on any specific app. They call this their "Digital Wellbeing Initiative." The average American spends nearly two hours per day distracted by social media. Two hours! That time is spread between all the different apps people use—Facebook Twitter, Instagram, YouTube, Snapchat, etc. Now, obviously, we live in a world where many people are actively on Social Media for work, that's not what I'm talking about here. What I'm talking about is wasted time. The mindless scrolling, the robotic 'liking,' the endless filter adjustments. When you think about two hours in a single day, it doesn't seem like that big a deal. But when you add up the monthly time expense, we're talking about a full week's worth of productivity spent on social media.

Now I'm not trying to say that social media is the enemy, because in reality, social media and digital communication often give us the ability to communicate with people that we otherwise would not be able to. The internet, after all, is a tool. This tool has the ability to deliver digital information faster than we can imagine, but it also has the ability to take away our desire to be present with people who are physically around us. This tool has the ability to overwrite our motivation to achievement. All the while, the notifications, the "likes," the vibrations, and the sounds are giving us blasts of dopamine, a hormone in our brain that was designed to alert us that we were doing something good for ourselves. This blast of dopamine makes us feel good, so we tend to seek out more of the thing or the behavior that caused that dopamine release. This is the physiological foundation of addiction.

Another result from the prevalence of digital media is our reduced patience. If you are old enough to remember when the internet first came into American homes in the early 1990s,[29] you remember having to wait to connect to the internet; you remember having to wait to load pages on the World Wide Web. In fact, you're probably thinking of the dial-up connection sound your 56k modem used to make after the dial tone. (In case you want to feel nostalgic, visit www.EricMBailey.com/sounds to hear that iconic dial up modem connection sound.) You remember having to wait for search results to load (in the days before Google). You remember having to wait for hours to download a document or a music file. You remember having to wait a lot. Today, if a web page takes more than a few seconds to load, you probably switch to a different task, so you don't have to wait. You might even open a new browser tab or simply feel frustrated.

This phenomenon of keeping multiple tabs open is a powerful analogy for society's current relationship with technology. With multiple tabs open, you always have something to look at but never an opportunity to just stop and think. Why? You've always got something to consume! You and everyone else using a computer or a smartphone have created a world ripe with distraction—and the cognitive cost of distraction to our interactions with real people is greater than we can comprehend. Frequently you see people driving slower than the speed limit and dipping out of their lane of traffic, all because they are distracted by technology. What is the impact of technology distraction at work? For example, if you fail to acknowledge a co-worker when they say "good morning," or when someone speaks to you, you take an extra second or two to respond because you're reading an email. Distraction reduces our cognitive abilities.

Date Night Debate

I would like to share a personal story with you. I am an introvert. Remember an introvert is someone who gains energy in solitude. Often, being among large groups of people drains the energy of an introvert like me. My wife, on the other hand, is an extrovert. Extroverts are people who do a majority of their thinking outside of their brains. An extrovert is someone who gains energy by being amid large groups of people. In our consulting firm, Bailey Strategic Innovation Group, I'm responsible for traveling around the country delivering keynote presentations, facilitating communication retreats, and delivering training. All among large groups of people. My wife is the Chief Financial Officer and Chief of Operations. She is responsible for running the business side of the business. I admit it's a little backwards to have the intro-vert doing the talking among people, and the extrovert doing the thinking at the computer, but we make it work.

Let's say it's a Friday, and I've been facilitating a full day strategic planning retreat for an organization. This particular Friday happens to be one of the several on which my wife and I will hire a babysitter and make space for a date night. The only thing to do is decide what we should do for our date. After a long day of office work for her, of course she wants to go out dancing! But after a long day of facilitating, I do not want to go out dancing. I would rather stay at home and watch Netflix on the couch. This is typically the point where our conversation takes a sharp turn and becomes an argument.

We find ourselves arguing the merits of her idea versus my idea. We find ourselves in the middle of a debate.

When people debate, we usually debate the ideas, not the reasoning behind our ideas. We debate the process, or the method—not the purpose. In his best-selling book *Start with Why*, Simon Sinek says, "People don't buy what you do, they buy why you do it."[30] When we get caught in debate, whether about what to do for date night or which sales technique to use to boost revenue, we usually neglect to share the WHY of our idea because each of us in the debate spends so much time focused on proving that our ideas is the right idea. In order to resolve a debate, we need to learn, instead, to first identify our mutual purpose and then develop our ideas from there. We need to work together to identify where our "Why" is aligned and make that "Why" the foundation of the rest of our conversation.

To find a mutual purpose in the middle of a debate, you can ask yourself two questions: first, "What do I truly want?" Now, for me, the easy, tempting way to answer that question during our date night debate is to say, "I want to watch Netflix." But that's not what I truly want—watching Netflix is just the first idea that I thought of to achieve my purpose. You might be saying, "No, seriously, Eric, Netflix is really what I want to do!" For everyone that says that, think about what you watch for the first several minutes of turning on Netflix. If you're not in the middle of binge-watching a show, opening Netflix can turn rapidly from a five-second task to a fifteen-minute exercise in scrolling past all of the things that you're *not* going to watch. Netflix is not what I truly want. It's just the first or possibly the easiest solution that I could think of.

A quick word of warning: If the answer to the question, "What do I really want" is "I want to win," I strongly advise you to stop talking. Cease and desist immediately. When you find yourself in the middle of a debate, and you notice you're trying to win the conversation, you will likely end up saying things you regret—things the other person will resent hearing. Remember, if you are trying to win, you are trying to make someone else lose. And the relationship (personal or professional) is not better for having a loser in it.

So do a quick check: If you are trying to win, take a break and have the conversation later. Any frustration or damage that comes from pausing the conversation is not nearly as bad as the fallout from saying something you'll regret.

Now back to my date night debate with the woman I love. First question: What is it that I truly want? Well, I want to spend time with my wife. Additionally, since I'm an introvert, I would like to spend time in a quiet environment so that I can recharge my energy. I would prefer not to have to interact with a lot of people. Watching Netflix accomplishes this, but it's not the only solution.

The second question I recommend asking to find a mutual purpose is, "What does the other person truly want?" Answering this question is going to require a bit of empathy. So, the better you know and understand someone, the better you will be at answering this question. On occasion, you simply won't know or can't figure out what someone truly wants. In that case, you're always welcome to ask. "It seems like we're stuck in a debate. I don't think I took the time to understand why you're so passionate about your idea, but I would like to." Caution: I hear people try to do this by asking the question like this: "Why do you care so much about going dancing?" Remember from chapter two that "why" can be born out of either judgment or curiosity. In this case, I am in the throes of a debate and my wife's brain is likely still tied up in the rightness of her idea (and the wrongness of my idea). When she hears me ask "why?" she is likely to perceive judgment. One way to approach asking this why question of the other person is to make sure the other person understands that you're asking out of genuine curiosity by saying something like, "Okay, I'm going to let go of my idea, but I want to understand your idea more. I want to know why going dancing is the right idea for you." After asking this way, I found that my wife wanted to be out of the house, among people, and most importantly, she wanted to spend time with me!

Let's see if we can find mutual purpose between the two of us. I want to spend time with my wife, I want to be in a quiet environment, and I want to recharge my energy. She wants to spend time with me, she wants to be among people, and she wants to be out of the house. Only when both of us let go of our method for achieving what we wanted, can we actually do the creative work necessary to find a mutually beneficial solution. In the scenario between me and my wife, it's clear that we want to spend time together, but I want to be in a quiet environment, and she wants to be outside of the house among people. At this point, it became clear to us that there was a way we could accomplish all of this. We went to the movies. We were in a quiet environment, among people, out of the house, and most importantly, we were spending time together. A fringe benefit from this solution is that after the two-hour movie, I had regained my energy a bit, so we went to an ice cream shop and just sat and talked for an hour eating our ice cream.

The lesson here is that debate often locks you deeper into your ideas and reduces your ability to identify mutual purpose. More often than not, when you're debating something, you and the other person are debating the merits of an idea rather than discussing the purpose behind it. When you stay at the level of ideas, you restrict your ability to find common desired results, saying things to each other like, "How could you possibly. . . ," or "I cannot believe that you would. . . ." Fortunately, almost any debate can be solved by finding mutual purpose. Mutual Purpose, The Solution for Debate is the 15th Principle of Human Understanding. Once you find that mutual purpose, you can commit to doing the work to come up with a creative solution. As much as each of us wants to believe there's only one solution to a problem (our solution!), there are actually an infinite number of solutions to a problem. But you and most other people usually get locked into one of the first reasonable ideas that you have and begin selling that idea in a debate. If your goal is to solve problems, it's clear that debate is a distraction that reduces your ability to solve problems.

I Never Finish Anythi... The Myth of Multitasking

In the 1990s, a buzzword erupted through the business world. As computers, cell phones, and other technology became more commonplace, the "effective executive" became an expert at "multitasking." For the next couple of decades, "multitasking" adorned the headlines of dozens of magazines. The prevailing notion was that to be most effective at work, you needed to be able to manage many tasks simultaneously. Multitasking usually meant typing a memorandum, handling a phone call, and reading the newspaper, all while clipping your toenails. Okay, maybe that last one wasn't part of it.

The word "multitasking" was added to the Oxford English Dictionary in 2003, the same year as "MP3," but its first use was back in 1965 in reference to an IBM computer that could process multiple tasks at the same time. In 1965, a computer that could do two things at the same time was considered revolutionary. By the 2000s, this wave of multitasking spread across the United States and the rest of the business world. In a 2002 article published by *Fast Company*, Allison Overholt instructed ambitious business people about "how to manage to stay sane when you're insanely busy . . . become very good at multitasking."[31] As more and more articles like this were published and more top executives shared their "secrets of success," people looked for new ways to achieve more things in less time.

Researchers and scientists, however, found that given how our brains work, multitasking actually is not possible. Furthermore, the attempt at multitasking, the practice that many of us were doing at that time, actually slows us down from achieving all of the tasks. In 1995, researchers Robert D. Rogers and Stephen Monsell showed that switching tasks, even if they are predictable, causes a measurable decline in reaction time.[32] If you add up the time it would take to do all the tasks individually and compare that to the time it takes to get them all done while multitasking, multitasking would prove to be significantly slower. The research suggests that this happens because your brain is not built to multitask. While you believe that you're multitasking, you're actually not doing the tasks at the same time. According to his 2011 article in *Psychology Today*, Jim Taylor PhD, explains that we are actually doing part of one activity, switching to the next, then doing part of that activity, switching back, and so on. Dr. Taylor calls this "serial tasking."[33] In other words, you do one task and then another task and then another task in rapid succession. Essentially, you're doing them in a series, rather than doing multiple tasks at the same time, thus giving you the illusion that you are multitasking. This process of serial tasking is slower because of all of the time, energy, and cognitive resources spent when you have to switch tasks. And as you invite distraction, you also increase your risk of error. This Myth of Multitasking is the sixteenth Principle of Human Understanding.

If multitasking is slower, why did it sweep through the business world? First, not everything that the business world does makes sense. Seriously, if you think about people at work, they are **attempting** to get work done. Additionally, there is pressure to **look as if** they are getting work done. Sometimes their main goal in the day is to maintain the appearance of being busy. When you see someone multitasking, although the tasks may be getting done more slowly, the person appears significantly busier. Then you hear them in the break room talking about how busy they are and how many projects they have going on at the same time.

Earlier in the chapter, I talked about how distraction reduces your cognitive ability. If you want to actually get projects done and get work done, you need to reduce distraction as much as possible. I urge you to cut the practice of multitasking so that you can get more done in less time, be more efficient and more effective, and be the hero at work. And you can leave your nail clippings at home.

By the way, research about multitasking and serial tasking didn't end in the 1990s. Researchers from the very next decade found that the reports of the death of multitasking had been greatly exaggerated.

So, Wait, Multitasking Is Real?

In 2017, PhD Psychologist Art Markman reignited the multitasking-serial tasking debate.[34] When studying the brain, he found that we actually *can* multitask in one very specific way. His research indicated that different tasks require different amounts of working memory (If you're a geek like me, think of RAM on a computer). Working memory is just the amount of information that we can hold in our mind at a given time. The Language Center of our brain handles all our speech, speech recognition, and thinking about words. Right now, as you read this book, your language center is active because you're reading words. Reading requires significant amounts of working memory. Discovering that working memory is responsible for accomplishing tasks enabled Dr. Markman to find the one way in which multitasking is possible. But before I can explain it, I need to first explain the distinction between what you don't know you know, versus what you know you know.

What You Don't Know You Know

Let me introduce a framework based on Martin Broadwell's "four levels of teaching" model,[35] that I call the "Conscious Competence Matrix." There are things that you know and things that you don't know in relation to competence / skill. Also, when it comes to consciousness or awareness, there are things that you know and things that you do not know. If the measures of consciousness are lined up along the horizontal axis of a chart, and the measures of competence are lined up on the vertical axis, we end up with a four-quadrant grid shown here.

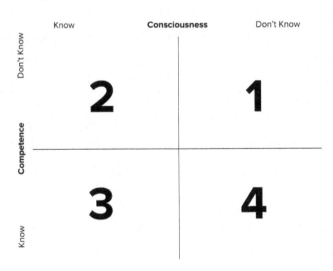

When you read out the four quadrants of the chart, you can see how the consciousness and competence overlap one another. The first box, in the upper right, is where we find things that you don't know that you know. Things at which you are unconsciously competent or unconsciously skilled. For most people in the United States, an example would be driving. Most adults have driven so many miles for so long that many of the tasks required for driving don't require thought because they are stored in your unconscious ability. This explains why sometimes you can drive down the freeway on your commute home and realize that you don't remember the last five minutes of your drive. This happens all the time because you have offloaded the cognitive resources for driving into your unconscious brain. This is also why sometimes when you're driving on the weekend to a place that's in the same direction of the office, you reflexively get off at the exit for work, even though it isn't the correct exit. Our automatic brain is the strongest in Box 1. What is the answer to 2+2? I assume you don't need to even think about the solution to that math problem before the answer presents itself to you seemingly instantaneously. Because you're so practiced at simple math, you can process it unconsciously. Many of the biases discussed in the previous chapter live in Box 1. When athletes get an element of their sport into Box 1, they call it "Flow." They stop thinking about what they're trying to accomplish and can just do it because their brain is so locked into that process.

Stephan Curry, one of the best shooters in the history of the National Basketball Association, is known widely for his uncanny three-point shooting ability. He can reliably fire off seemingly impossible shots from thirty-five feet, well beyond the three-point line. But what makes Stephan a truly incredible threat is his nearly perfect free-throw shooting percentage. Not only is he is the best free-throw shooter currently in the NBA, with a career average better than nine makes per ten attempts, he is the best free throw shooter in the history of the NBA. Free throws are awarded for violations committed by the opposing team, and uncontested "free" shots can drastically change the outcome of a basketball game. But even though free-throws are simple, throughout the entire history of the NBA, the average free throw percentage has been a little north of seven out of every ten shots. Why? Because free throws are not only physical, they're mental. The pace of the game changes and all eyes lock on the shooter. Since the beginning of the NBA, the free throw average has been roughly the same, and yet Steph scores an extra twenty points per one hundred attempts. With over 2,000 made free throws in his career, Steph Curry has managed to put making free throws into Box 1. He doesn't need to think; he just does it. When considering any new skill, getting it into unconscious competence (Box 1) is the goal.

Box 2 on the upper left holds all the things that we know that we know. It's the conscious competence box—things that we know we are skilled at. These are things like doing long division or parallel parking a car. You can do it—you know how to do it—but sometimes it may be a little difficult, and you have to concentrate to get it done. Now I understand that some people put doing long division and parallel parking into a different box because they know that they can't do them, but the point is that these things in Box 2 typically don't happen on autopilot. However, I do know some people who have automatic parallel parking as a feature in their vehicle. I'm not sure what box that should go in.

What is the cubed root of 27? Honestly think about it. I'm sure you can get it. What number times itself and then times itself again equals 27? For most people, the answer to this math problem is in your Box 2. The answer's not as automatic as 2+2, but you know it's in there somewhere.

Now we go south of the horizontal axis and things start to get interesting. Box 3 is for things that we know that we don't know—things at which we are consciously incompetent. For example, I am perfectly aware that I don't know the first thing about rocket science. While I am a geek, and I do love watching rocket launches, and I have gone to a lecture by astrophysicist Neil deGrasse Tyson, I have no idea what it takes to get a spacecraft into orbit. I don't even know what kind of math you would need to use to accomplish those feats. So yes, I do enjoy rockets, and I admire the science that it takes to get rockets into the sky, but I'm fully aware of my incompetence at rocket science. Box 3 is a powerful box because it holds all the things that you know that you can learn. If you're reading this book, I hope that you're identifying several things that you now have the opportunity to learn. Remember, the only things in life that we can learn are things that we don't yet know. That is why the lower half of this chart is so important. Growth happens at the bottom of the chart. In fact, in the second episode of his 2014 television show *Cosmos: A Spacetime Odyssey*, Neil deGrasse Tyson said, "Science works on the frontier between knowledge and ignorance. We're not afraid to admit what we don't know. There's no shame in that. The only shame is to pretend that we have all of the answers." Exploring Box 3 is truly a great opportunity, so long as we understand the difference between Box 3 and Box 4.

Box 4 is the danger box. Box 4 is full of the things that we don't know that we don't know. We are unconscious of our incompetence about them, and we're unaware that we are unskilled. I have no examples to put into Box 4 because clearly there is nothing that I don't know I don't know. If I don't know that I don't know these things, I can't put them into the box. But don't worry, I'll give you some examples.

If you've ever been a boss, you've had to deliver feedback to somebody. Every once in a while, you gave someone feedback about something that they were unskilled at, and they didn't know that they were unskilled at it. You may have been the first one to ever point this out to them. Think about what their reaction was to that feedback. Often people get upset or offended—typical symptoms of being defensive. It's important to understand that when people are reacting in this way, they are not necessarily reacting to you. They're reacting to the exposure of their Box 4. Everyone deals with being exposed in different ways. That's why when you deliver feedback, it's critical to pay attention to how people are receiving the feedback. Are they taking it as a condemnation of who they are, or are they taking it as a judgment of what they have done? Science has indicated that the most successful feedback hits people in the place of what they have done, and the least successful feedback hits people in the place of who they are.[36] Where feedback lands for another person is a result of the delivery as well as the reception.

People with higher resilience tend to appreciate critical feedback because they find it's more likely going to help them improve. It's also likely they have more experience exploring their Box 4. The only way that we can learn things in our Box 4 is from observation and feedback. Either we have an experience that brings into focus something that we were previously unaware of, OR someone gives us feedback. While I cannot explain something that is in my Box 4, I can give you an example of how an item in my Box 4 reared its ugly head and burst its way into Box 3.

One day my wife came to me and said, "Do you realize that you say the word 'appreciate' wrong?"

"What do you mean?" I asked her. "Are you saying that I say "a-pri-**sh**-ee-ate"?

"No," she told me. "You don't mess up the "sh" sound. You miss the "ee" sound. "The word is 'a-PREESH-ee-ate' and you pronounce it "a-PRISH-ee-ate." My first reaction was abject denial. "How could you possibly think that I'm saying it wrong? I've said it this way my entire life!" I did not enjoy this feedback at all because for my entire life, I believed that I was saying the word correctly. It turned out that I wasn't, at least according to my wife. . . and Merriam-Webster. Honestly, it took me several days of this conversation with my wife to actually believe her and learn that I was, in fact, saying it wrong. Once I became conscious of that fact, it moved from Box 4 to Box 3. From unconscious incompetence to conscious competence. I knew that I was saying it wrong, but I still struggled with saying it right. This is so uncomfortable to share in the book, but I felt like a child as I played with different emphases on different syllables. I swapped "EE" sounds for "I" sounds and probably added a couple of sounds that shouldn't belong anywhere near that word. But for a while, I was trying to say the word "appreciate" as much as possible. And every time that I did, my wife would giggle. She says that she was giggling because it was cute that I was working so hard, but I perceived that she was giggling because I kept saying it wrong. It was only through the journey of moving from Box 4 to Box 3 that I can now say that I *appreciate* my wife for helping me reach Box 2.

The goal of all learning and development is to move from Box 4 to Box

3, Box 3 to Box 2, and Box 2 to Box 1. The process of moving from Box 4 to Box 3 happens through observation and feedback from your spouse. Okay, not always your spouse, but through observation and feedback. This transition is the hardest because as you become aware of what you do not know, ego gets in the way. The Illusion of Certainty and the Fight for Right have to step aside before you can acknowledge that there is something to learn. When my wife told me that I was saying that word wrong, it took me quite a while to hear what she was saying and even longer to accept that she might possibly be right. I fully understand that there may be some nuanced dialect differences between appr-ee-shiate and appr-i-shiate because we are from different parts of the country, like saying route or route, or data and data, but in this situation, I didn't even know there was a different way to say it. I never even heard my wife saying it different from the way I was saying it. Funny brain tangent . . . Isn't it interesting that you read the words data and data with two different pronunciations? The power of perception. Okay, back to work.

The transition from Box 3 to Box 2 happens through training. When there's a skill that you currently do not possess but want to acquire, you go to a workshop, training course, seminar, or download an app. You train in the skill so that you can become competent in it. The final transition, from Box 2 to Box 1 happens through deliberate practice. Keep in mind, however, that "Practice makes perfect" isn't completely true. Perfect practice makes perfect. Stephan Curry is as perfect of a free throw shooter as any NBA player has ever been. Coaches and sports announcers will often say that he's "automatic" from the free throw line. How did he get so close to perfect?

Many high school basketball coaches make their players practice free throws during every practice. I know of a couple of coaches that say that players cannot leave until they have made ten free throws. They know that games are often won (or lost) at the free throw line, so they want their players to have the best chance possible by making them practice and practice and practice. I bet that by the time a player makes it to the NBA or WNBA they have shot well over 10,000 practice free throws, and yet the average free throw accuracy is still between seventy and seventy five percent.

Steph Curry takes a different approach to practicing free throws. It's not that he employs hundreds of fans to distract him while he practices, but his definition of success is much more exact than anyone else. When he finishes his practice, Steph gives himself the same goal of making ten free throws, but he adds a couple of adjustments. His goal is not only to make ten, but to make ten in a row. What's more, he gave himself the added target of swishing at least half of them. A swish is a shot where the ball, with a diameter of 12 inches, makes it through the rim with a diameter of 18 inches, without touching the rim at all. The word "swish" is onomatopoeia, named for the sound the net makes as the ball swishes through without touching the rim.

So not only does Steph practice his free throws after practice, but he has to make ten free throws in a row. If he misses one, he starts over. Not only does he have to make ten in a row, but if the ball touches any part of the rim on six or more of the made shots, he starts over. Perfect practice makes perfect. Because of this practice, the apex of Steph Curry's shot arc is over 12 inches higher than the average shooter. Steph Curry does not need to think about his free throws because he has done it perfectly so many times. His free throw is automatic. Even when fans from opposing teams are screaming at him and doing everything possible to cause a distraction, Steph is not worried because free throws for him land solidly in Box 1.

Multitasking Redux

The purpose of discussing the "Conscious Competence Matrix" is to understand the new science of multitasking. Brain scientists discovered that when we execute a task in Box 1 (Unconscious Competence), we are working with our unconscious brain, leaving our cognitive resources available to do other tasks simultaneously. This is why we are capable of texting while driving. Typically when I mention texting and driving, a lot of people get really uncomfortable, as if I am advocating for texting and driving. To be 100 percent clear, I'm not. What I am saying is that this research explains the reason that we are *able* to text and drive. Just because it can be done, doesn't mean that it should be done. There are still significant cognitive problems with texting while driving.

In a scenario in which you are texting and driving, you can offload the task of driving to your unconscious brain Because as we discussed earlier, for most adults, driving is so baked into habit that we can do it without thinking. It is in our Box 1. This leaves more cognitive resources available for texting. The problem arises when the driving task requires your cognitive awareness again. This can happen if there is an unexpected curve in the road, a set of brake lights in front of you, or a child in front of your vehicle. All those things require you to do actions that are outside the typical unconscious driving, Box 2 actions. These are actions that you can do, but you cannot do passively. If your cognitive awareness is occupied by texting or using your phone for another purpose, there will be a delay in reaction time as you switch from one task to another. In time, that delay could cost tremendous physical damage, emotional damage, or loss of life. It's not important that it can be done without incident 999 times, because the impact of the *one* time it doesn't work is critical and could be deadly.

Other common, and less controversial examples of Box 1 multitasking are brushing your teeth while reading the news, drinking coffee while checking your email, or jogging on a treadmill while listening to an audiobook. You'll notice that all these examples include two tasks that are controlled by different parts of the brain. One involves the language center (reading, talking, listening) and the other involves some routine physical activity. When you try to simultaneously achieve two tasks that require your language center, you'll find that you simply slow down because of distraction.

Why Girls Aren't Good at Math

I want to quickly get this out in the open—the title of the section has nothing to do with my opinion (or reality for that matter), but it has everything to do with surprising research about societal myths and how they can manifest into actual educational outcomes. This research from Sian Beilock explores how perception can cause distraction and cause lower test scores.[37]

In the United States, it has been long believed, albeit erroneously, that girls are not as strong as boys in the subjects of math, science, and engineering. Time and time again, test results confirmed that this was true. When normalized for external factors like socio-economic differences and work ethic, boys and girls would perform differently on math tests. Boys and girls who get similar grades and homework scores don't do the same on math tests. Why was this the case? Beilock's research found that girls performed worse on average than boys because they believed they would. Because of the shared social understanding that girls were not as strong in math as boys, they did worse on exams. But good news, because this phenomenon is psychologically driven, it can be reversed relatively easily.

Research by Walton, Logel, Peach, Spencer, and Zanna found that of the methods that counteracted this effect was telling girls, "On this specific kind of test, girls significantly outperform boys." Even though the actual test was exactly the same, the outcome was remarkable. Rather than underperforming, girls performed the same if not slightly higher than boys. Similar interventions were done with minority students (who similarly underperform on tests).[38] In this study, rather than saying that minority students would outperform majority students on a specific test, researchers didn't say that the students were taking a test. Instead, they called it either a puzzle or an exercise. When they did that, rather than underperforming, minority students performed significantly better and on par with the rest of their peers.

But why did girls perform poorly on math tests to begin with? Researchers determined that there is a singular moment during a difficult math problem that social understanding becomes tremendously problematic for girls. Typically, without the social understanding that girls perform worse at math than boys, girls will dedicate a certain period of time to accomplishing a difficult problem. Beilock found that during the most difficult math problems, girls' internal dialogue about their abilities in relation to boys' ability actually distracts them from focusing on a difficult math problem. That distraction, discussed earlier in this chapter, reduces girls' cognitive ability in that moment. When this happens, girls will devote less time to those difficult problems because of the distraction of their social understanding. When the test is introduced in a different way, however, without the social understanding, that distraction is not present, or is less present, and girls have more cognitive resources available to overcome difficult problems.

When we talk about distraction, we often focus on technology and the other things that distract us. It's more important, however, to identify how other kinds of social distraction play a powerful role in the way that we live our lives. Think about how people behave when they're distracted. They make seemingly irrational decisions that are not fully informed by the environment around them. People in the office, for example, might not say "Hi" in the morning because they're distracted by the stress of an upcoming meeting. Then their lack of greeting starts other people's Perception Escalator, which can erode relationships. Think about why people get distracted. If you understand that an employee works in an environment ripe for distraction, maybe you can do the work to discover what they need to thrive. Maybe it's knowledge, maybe it's desire, maybe it's passion, or maybe it's significance. Rather than allowing someone else's distraction to take you down the path of saying things like, "How could you possibly?" you can use your knowledge of social distraction to better understand and motivate co-workers or employees.

Knowing that social understanding, or any other external context, can become a distraction for people, you also now know that those distractions can negatively impact employees' overall performance. With that understanding, a boss might ask, "What negative social understandings may exist for my employees? What can I do to reduce the impact of these negative social understandings? How can I leverage certain social understandings to improve the working experience of my employees?" Please be aware that this conversation can be tremendously important but also has the potential to be very sensitive.

To go back and answer the question, "Why are girls bad at math?" The answer is . . . they aren't. Social understanding creates conditions for girls (*and* boys) to believe that girls are bad at math. Unfortunately, some girls do poorly on math tests simply because they are aware of this myth. If we can change girls' beliefs about girls' abilities, we can change the statistics. Similarly, if leaders can better understand the distractions their employees face and give them training and tools to manage those distractions, their employees can change their work environment. If employees become aware that their own perceptions can impede success, they can intentionally change the way they see themselves. Imagine what would happen if we were collectively unleashed from negative social understanding. We would change the world.

A New Way to Think about Stereotypes

According to Beilock, worrying about social expectations, especially if they are negative expectations, is called "Stereotype Threat."[39] This concept affects people in different ways, but essentially, it occurs when you become aware of a stereotype about a group that you belong to. Then, aware of the stereotype, you change your behavior to either counteract or minimize the manifestation of that stereotype. Often, modifying your behavior is counterproductive, resulting in you reinforcing the stereotype. For example, if you believe that other people see the group you're a member of as stupid or unintelligent, you might work harder to project that you are intelligent. This extra effort is outside of your normal behavior and may cause you to stumble on your words, not being able to speak in fluid sentences, or not being able to respond appropriately to questions. When this happens, people who you are attempting to have a conversation with may conclude that you are not intelligent. Stereotype Threat is one of the many ways that we can distract ourselves by focusing on the perceptions of other people. This is the effect at play when girls sit down to a math test.

The opposite of the Stereotype Threat is the "Stereotype Tax," which occurs when you become aware of the stereotypes that other people hold about you or a group that you're a member of and then you use the expectation of those stereotypes to your advantage. For example, if a services vendor believes that I am unintelligent, and I begin negotiating a price, they may lean on their belief about how unintelligent people would behave in negotiation. I can use that knowledge to my advantage, playing up the signals that I am unintelligent, and then using my actual intelligence to get a better deal in the negotiation. These Stereotype Expectations (Stereotype Threat and Stereotype Tax) make up Principle 17 and bring me to Annie Duke.

The Duchess

Shankar Vedantam is a journalist for National Public Radio and author of the book *The Hidden Brain: How Our Unconscious Minds Elect Presidents, Control Markets, Wage Wars, and Save Our Lives*. He also hosts a podcast and radio show called *The Hidden Brain*. In his book and his podcast, Vedantam dives into the psychology just below the surface of human behavior. Just as I attempt to do in my work, Vedantam has a way of making the seemingly complex psychology accessible to lay people. If you haven't yet had the opportunity to check out his work, visit www.HiddenBrain.com. While all his work is powerful, my favorite is the story he tells about how Annie Duke, the first female Grand Champion of the World Series of Poker, leveraged stereotypes to walk away with $2,000,000. Before Annie Duke, there were very few women in professional poker. Poker was seen as a men's game. The social understanding was that women didn't have the temperament or the ability to be successful poker players.

In 2004, Annie Duke earned her spot in the very first World Series of Poker Tournament of Champions, an invitation-only tournament with the year's best poker players. Throughout her career, Annie was almost always the only female at the table. Very quickly she realized that other people around her assumed she couldn't play, meaning she couldn't bet or bluff—she was just a pretty face. And yet, Annie moved her way through the rankings and was invited to the Tournament of Champions, an all-star event in which each of ten poker players tried to wipe out their opponents by taking all their money.

As Annie sat down at the champion table, she became hyper aware of stereotypes about women in poker. Because of her awareness, she attempted to compensate. In poker, when you overcompensate it is typically emotional and you are not focused on your normal style of play. Annie admitted that she made several poor decisions, because she was aware of the stereotypes against women poker players. Annie played worse during the Tournament of Champions because she was aware of the stereotypes. For her opponents, these poor decisions confirmed the stereotypes.

During a break, however, Annie realized that the play that she was exhibiting was not to her standard. She was down several thousands of dollars in chips and needed to recalibrate. She leaned on her experience of playing poker successfully and how she cut through the stereotypes. You see, this championship table wasn't the first poker table that Annie had played at. In fact, she had built a career of breaking through stereotypes. Originally, Annie was encouraged to play poker by her brother Howard Lederer, who is also a professional poker player and World Series of Poker champion. In 1992, Lederer sent Annie $2,400 and some poker theory books, encouraging her to play professionally. Annie honed her skills at the Crystal Lounge in Billings, Montana, and in 1994, she entered her first World Series of Poker event in Las Vegas. Within her first month, Annie ultimately won over $70,000. Annie continued to thrive in poker over the years, winning the World Series of Poker Tournament in Omaha, Nebraska in 2004. This win gave Annie the invitation to the first ever Tournament of Champions.

What did Annie do to thrive in poker despite the stereotypes against women players? Just like a champion poker player, she started to pay close attention to fine details. She began to notice all the different stereotypes that the other players had about her and started categorizing them. She categorized the first type as the "flirting chauvinist." These were the men who thought of her as nothing more than proverbial "eye candy" with no real reason to be there other than to look pretty. This type of player would hold the chair for her, calm her, call her "darling," "sweetheart," "doll," or other words designed to put her in a lower power position. Annie leveraged this type by subtly flirting with them. She obviously never actually went on any dates with them, nor did she want to—she just leveraged their perception of her to distract them from their play. It worked.

The second category she labeled the "disrespecting chauvinist." These were men who thought of her as being entirely incapable of playing well. This is the type that would actively say things to the table about her, to indicate exactly how insignificant they thought she was. They would comment on every bad move she made, appending the comment with something to the effect of, "because girls can't play." She leveraged this type by bluffing them. They didn't know how to handle her. They didn't think that she *could* bluff, so they didn't believe that she *would* bluff.

The third category were the "angry chauvinists." This category of player would do anything to avoid being beaten by a "girl." In poker, if you have a strong hand, you bet a lot of money. If you bet too much, other players might get scared and fold their hand (giving up for that hand). If you don't have a strong hand, you can bluff (lie) by betting a lot of money. When someone makes a bet, you can either "call" the bet, by betting the same amount, "raise" the bet by betting even more money, or fold. Annie noticed that the "angry chauvinists" would "call" every single bet, so she couldn't bluff them. They would frequently bluff her because there was nothing more gratifying than bluffing the girl and having her fold and then showing that they had a weak hand, proving that "girls were easy to fool," reinforcing their stereotype. Knowing these angry chauvinist types, Annie would just be patient and strike when the time was right, allowing them to "impale them-selves on her chips." One of the top-rated poker players in the world, Phil Hellmuth, was an angry chauvinist type. At that time, he held a handful of world championships. What she did to tax his stereotype was to continually confound him. He believed that she could not bluff, so she bluffed him. He believed that when she won, she was getting lucky. Annie put on the act that she was getting lucky—and kept winning. Every single time she would win, it would infuriate him, throwing him more off his game. Ultimately, in the final hand, Phil could be heard talking to himself, trying to figure out how Annie was beating him.

Watching the replay is tremendously entertaining, even though watching it all as it happened live was incredibly tense, and somewhat embarrassing for Phil. Ultimately, Annie won the tournament after setting a trap for Phil. Once it was revealed that Annie won, Phil Hellmuth had a meltdown. In the video, he paces back and forth in the hallways swearing and going absolutely nuts because he can't figure out how she won. You can see the video of the final hand between Annie and Phil, including his meltdown by visiting www. EricMBailey.com/poker

The lesson to learn from Annie Duke is to not allow yourself to fall into Stereotype Threat, because just like any other distraction, Stereotype Threat can reduce your cognitive ability to be effective at work—or at poker. The social understandings that other people hold around you, or around your groups and teams, are nothing more than perceptions. These perceptions can prove to be a distraction from achievement and from being fully present. Being present is a crucial element of the human experience.

Stop Being So Mousy

Have you ever sat down in someone's office for a meeting or a conversation and every five minutes and two seconds, she moves her hand to her mouse or trackpad and wiggles it? Why does she do that? She does it because her monitor just went black. She wants to make sure her computer doesn't go to sleep.

Let's think about the true impact of this behavior. Monitoring the screen and responding to changes takes her mentally away from you and your conversation. She's thinking about preventing her computer from going to sleep and briefly loses focus on what you're saying. Sometimes this gap is tangible, especially when she takes a second to realize you have just asked a question, or she takes a second to complete a word that she started saying. When these distractions happen, your Perception Escalator turns on. As you perceive this behavior, you begin telling or reinforcing stories about your importance. You begin to judge and create feelings. But let's go back to the impacts. What is the impact of her NOT wiggling the mouse? She has to enter her password to unlock her computer, which is likely a time savings of less than two seconds. In effect, she's distracted and choosing to interrupt your thirty-minute conversation six times for a savings of two seconds. Now some of you reading this might be a mouse wiggler. I encourage you to let go of distraction and give your full cognitive resources to the person in front of you.

Samantha and Karl both experienced a lot of distractions from actually solving the problem. They were so caught up in the fight of the situation to even realize what they were trying to solve. With the powerful distraction of debate, they never looked for mutual purpose, even though it was there. What Karl truly wanted was to be respected and to share the responsibility of making coffee. What Samantha truly wanted was to be respected and to have coffee available in the afternoon. If they would have let go of their ideas and frustrations, they would have been able to find that mutual purpose and actually solve the problem. There are so many distractions in our daily lives that make us less efficient and effective. Whenever possible, we need to find ways to recalibrate to what we truly want. Then, we need to behave in ways that will help us toward achievement.

Principles of Human Understanding

The Observation Trap Principles

Can trap us by influencing the way we observe the world.

1. The Illusion of Certainty
2. Perception is More Important Than Reality
3. The Desire to Fight to Be Right
4. The Power of Distinction
5. Context is the Underlying Fabric by Which We Encounter the World
6. Empathy Changes Your Judgment

The Orientation Trap Principles

Can trap us by augmenting how we orient ourselves in the world.

7. The Truth About Bias
8. Understanding Fundamental Attribution Error (FAE)
9. The Insidious Nature of Joy from Pain
10. The Fluidity of Tribal Boundaries
11. The Validation of Truth

The Decision Trap Principles

Can trap us by leading us to make uninformed decisions.

12. The Truth About Judgment / Decisions
13. Just OODA It!
14. Cognitive Destruction from Distraction
15. Mutual Purpose, The Solution for Debate
16. The Myth of Multitasking
17. Stereotype Expectations

CHAPTER 6

Pattern Recognition

"There are patterns because we try to find them.
A desperate attempt at order because we can't face
the terror that it might all be random."

—Lauren Beukes

The human brain is tuned to identify patterns so that we can make sense of the world and attempt to accurately predict what is going to happen. A problem can arise when we lean too heavily on the assumption that the patterns that we see are consistent in perpetuity. Then our Illusion of Certainty kicks in, and we are left believing that the way we expect to see the world is the way that the world actually is. Take, for example, another powerful idea from Benjamin Franklin: "After reading and re-reading the the sentence at present, the the power of the the human brain and its function become the the most consistent points of failure. Then you realize the the word 'the' was repeated every single time." Okay, obviously this is not from Benjamin Franklin, but did you catch all the times that the word "the" was repeated? You may have caught one or two of the repeats, but most people read through this sentence and don't catch all five of the repeated "the's." This happens because of our ability to see what we expect to see—an amazing ability, as well as a tremendous liability for human beings at home and in the workplace.

Face It

Looking at the following images, what do you see?[40, 41, 42, 43, 44, 45]

If you're like most people, you identified faces in all of them. Why is that? There's actually a part of the human brain that's responsible for facial recognition. It's called the "fusiform gyrus." This part of the brain is active through infancy and becomes fully developed in adolescence. It gives us the uncanny ability to identify people simply by viewing their faces. Interestingly enough, according to brain scans, this part of the brain is also at work when we recognize faces in inanimate objects, like the images I've included here. Through a phenomenon called "pareidolia," our ability to identify shapes is so powerful, that we often perceive faces that are not there. An example is the man in the moon—or identifying faces or animals in the clouds. The word "pareidolia" comes from the Greek words Para (alternative) and eidōlon (image) and references the way in which we can perceive different meanings in images in objects.

Pattern recognition and expectation is one of the underlying functions of bias. Remember, bias is "a systematic error in thinking that can impact our judgments and decision making." As I've mentioned before, bias isn't necessarily bad; neither is pattern recognition. However, it can lead our brains to find patterns in data or stimuli that cause us to draw conclusions that aren't necessarily there. In the breakroom, for example, Samantha and Karl both saw certain actions as aligned with patterns that each of them were already familiar with. For Samantha, Karl's accented hand motions and elevated tone of voice fit the pattern of someone preparing to fight. For Karl, Samantha's exasperated exhales whenever he made a point, fit the pattern of someone who is stubborn and unwilling to listen.

Likewise, bosses recognize patterns of behavior all the time and make important decisions based on those patterns. I once had a professor at Arizona State University who told us about his secret for hiring the best people. As future members of the workforce, we all leaned in to learn his secret. "When any interview was over, I always looked at the backs of the shoes of the interviewee," he said. "If the shoes were wrinkled in the back, that told me the interviewee doesn't take the time to untie their shoes or use a shoehorn, which means they're disorganized and likely won't be a good hire." The entire class was stunned. We didn't believe stepping into shoes and not using a shoehorn would necessarily indicate that someone wouldn't be a good hire! And yet, this professor, who spent decades as a hiring manager, saw a pattern and used that pattern to make decisions.

Always remember that your ability to recognize patterns is not always based in the reality of the situation. Do not be afraid to challenge your initial assumptions.

Let's Use Patterns to Win Some Money

Erroneous pattern recognition plays out in what Psychologists call the "Gambler's Fallacy."[46] Imagine that you're sitting down in a casino at a roulette table in Europe. Since you might not know how the game of roulette works, I will briefly explain it. The game of roulette consists of a little white ball, a wheel, and a betting table. The wheel is spun on the table, similar to the spinner from the board game LIFE. Once the wheel is spinning, the ball is spun around an outside track and drops onto the wheel. Around the perimeter of the wheel, the ball can land in one of many different slots. The European version of this game has 37 slots; the American version has 38, but in this scenario, you're in Europe, so your ball can land in one of 37 slots. The slots are randomly labeled 1-36, with every slot alternating between red and black. In addition to the red and black 1-36, the game has an additional ZERO slot colored green.

When you bet, you can choose from many options. You can bet on specific numbers, number ranges, colors, etc. The introduction of the green zero drops the odds below 50/50, which is why, over time, the casino wins. But since there is nearly a 50 percent chance at winning, many betters decide to bet red or black. For this scenario, that's what you're going to do.

You walk into the casino and you observe a lot of hollering and excitement from a roulette table. You find an empty space at the table and ask, "What's all the excitement about?"

"The ball has landed on black the last six times," says the woman next to you.

What do you do? Of course, you'll break out your notebook and calculate the specific odds of landing on black six times in a row and marvel at the spectacle. I'm kidding— you're there to gamble. You join the quick rush of people betting on red. Surely the odds of hitting black seven times in a row is astronomical, and therefore, red must be coming! It's due. Nope. Black. Everyone erupts in what can only be described as an explosion of excitement, incredulity, and pure joy, which draws more attention. With so many people playing now, it takes several minutes to start the next spin.

As the dealer spins the ball around the track, dozens of hands try to get last minute bets on red, because what are the odds of black hitting eight times in a row? The dealer says, "no more bets" and the ball bounces around the wheel and lands on Black. Impossible. The result of the next 18 spins: Black. Black. Black. Black. Black. Black. Black. Black. Black. Black. Black. Black. Black. Black. Black. Black. Black. You, along with your table mates, lost millions of dollars betting against black, erroneously thinking that red (or green) was due. You knew the odds of such a long run of black meant that the chances were ever-increasing for a run of red. The odds of the roulette wheel landing on black twenty-six times in a row is something in the neighborhood of one in sixty-six million. And because the odds were so unlikely, with each result of black, you and your fellow gamblers bet more and more money.

Now, guess what? This is a true story. On August 18, 1913 at the Monte Carlo casino, gamblers at one roulette wheel lost millions of dollars because of an unbelievable run of black. With each result, gamblers became more certain that Red (or Green) would be next. How could it be possible that the ball would land on black twenty-six times in a row? Gamblers decided that it wasn't possible, and they bet against it happening.

The one thing that you and your fellow gamblers failed to consider is that nobody actually bet on black twenty-six times in a row. Each bet was a bet on the next spin. And each spin has the exact same odds. The American Psychology Association defines this as the Gambler's Fallacy: "A failure to recognize the independence of chance events, leading to the mistaken belief that one can predict the outcome of a chance event on the basis of the outcomes of past chance events." Yes, when you look back, you can calculate the odds of two or ten or eighteen or twenty-six in a row, but contrary to the behavior, there is no forward-looking bet for twenty-six in a row.

Whether we think about it or not, at work, we're constantly predicting what's going to happen, who is going to be late to their shift, who is going to speak up in the meeting. We use our perception of the world to create an ideal framework for the way that we expect people to think, react, respond, and behave. When people behave outside of these expected patterns, it can be so jarring, that it triggers FAE, and we judge that they're stupid. Just like in Monte Carlo, it was inconceivable that the ball would land on a black number that many times, so gamblers spent millions of dollars expecting a pattern that wasn't necessarily there.

Let's look at a fun way that you can leverage your co-workers' pattern expectations at the next office party!

Coin Flip Party Trick

If you are the type of person who loves to blow people's minds, you can do this party trick and be a hero for all eternity. All you need for supplies is a quarter (or any coin with two distinct sides), paper, and pens. What you want to do is give one sheet of paper and a pen to everyone participating and ask them to write their names on their paper and the numbers one through fifty down the left side. Let them know that you're going to leave the room. When you do, they should randomly select one person to be the official "Coin Flipper." Before the coin is flipped, everyone who is playing needs to predict the outcome of all fifty coin flips by writing heads or tails fifty times down their sheet of paper. Once everyone is done predicting, the Coin Flipper will then flip the coin fifty times and record each of his or her tosses on a paper with his or her name on top, just as the other participants have done.

After the coin flipping is finished, ask the Coin Flipper and participants to put their papers all in one pile and shuffle the order of the papers. When this process is finished, have someone let you know it's time to return. As soon as you return, leaf through all the papers. Then, as if you were a magician, you will quickly and correctly identify the person that was the Coin Flipper. Suddenly, you'll be known as a genius for all time (Or they'll revert to 1692 mob mentality and try you for being a witch, one of the two).

You might be thinking, "But Eric, how will I know which person flipped the coin?"

Great question. Just like with roulette in Monte Carlo, sometimes a string of 50/50 events produces long runs of one option. Most adults won't predict a long run of one side of the 50/50, so when you look through the sheets of paper, look for the one that has the longest runs of a single side. Remember, each coin flip has a 50/50 chance. In fact, in 100 coin flips, the chances of getting a run of six is over 54 percent! Most adults have a hard time trusting this fact and will estimate a run of two or maybe four of "heads" maximum.

As adults, we constantly perceive patterns, whether in the behavior of other people or in expectations of the world around us. Many times, these expected patterns lead us down the path of incorrect conclusions. Physicist and Science Education Guru Dereck Muller introduced the world to a fun game of patterns and assumptions that demonstrates the problem of incorrect conclusions. I would like to play his game with you. Here's how it works. I'm going to propose a series of numbers that follow a specific rule. To play, you only need to do two things. First, propose three additional numbers that you think fit the rule. Second, guess what the rule is. I'll let you know whether or not you guessed correctly.

Here is the series: 4, 8, 16 . . .

Based on this series, list in your head three more numbers that would fit the rule and identify what you believe the rule to be. If you're like most people, you're probably proposing something like 16, 32, and 64 or 8, 16, and 32. Both of those number sets fit the rule. The question is, what do you believe the rule is?

During Muller's version of the game, he surveyed dozens of people who said something like, "The rule is that you're doubling the number every time."

No, that's NOT the rule, and I'm not going to put you through the rest of the exercise. But I will explain what typically happens next in the interaction based on Muller's example. The typical response: "Yeah, but the numbers do double!" which is completely true, but that's not the rule. Then Muller asked them to identify three more numbers to identify the rule. Almost every participant proposed three more numbers that followed THEIR rule of doubling, which does *fit* the rule, but does not define the rule.

At this point, participants started to get a little frustrated because they believed that Muller was being stubborn. What they were not doing, however, was trying to identify Muller's rule. Instead, what they were doing was trying to prove that their idea about the rule was right. Each time he asked them to provide a set of numbers, they proposed numbers that doubled and concluded, "See! If those numbers fit the rule, the rule must be doubling!"

To discern the rule, what they actually needed to do was gain additional information about the rule. The failing method they took, however, was to continually propose numbers that validated what they already believed. This error in thinking is another manifestation of the Confirmation Bias that we talked about in Chapter Four: "We often look for evidence to confirm that which we already believe." The participants believed that the rule was doubling numbers, so each time they tested numbers, they proposed numbers that doubled even after Derek told them that the rule wasn't doubling numbers.

Remember that the only things in life that you can learn, are things that you don't yet know. To garner the highest amount of information, participants should have been proposing numbers that they thought would NOT fit the rule. Only then could they begin to close in on the rule itself. If they proposed three numbers that were NOT doubling, like 8, 16, 50, Muller would have said, "Yes, that fits the rule." If they proposed three more numbers like 1, 2, 3, he would have said, "Yes, that fits the rule." If they proposed three more numbers like 10, 8, 2, he would have said, "No, that does not fit the rule." At this point, most people have enough information to identify the rule: "Numbers in ascending order."

The reason that I like this game is that it illustrates two powerful human abilities—Pattern Recognition and Confirmation Bias. When these two abilities work in concert, human beings often come to incorrect conclusions. As humans, we easily get locked into ideas we believe are right, then work to confirm that those ideas were correct. This is what I call the Pull of Patterns, the eighteenth Principle of Human Understanding. Many disagreements turn into arguments because of pattern recognition in concert with confirmation bias.

Back in the office breakroom, for example, Samantha began to notice that Karl was punctuating his words with his hands, almost as if they were hatchets chopping at some invisible tree between the two of them. Still fueled by the word "animal" on the sign, which was now tightly crumpled in her hand, Samantha felt Karl's aggression. He was leaning in, almost standing over her, striking at the air as he spoke. For Samantha, she was certain that this guy was on the verge of screaming in her face, something she does not put up with. All the signs were there: his hands, the tone of his voice, his posture, his wild eyes; Samantha *knew* where this was going and was matching his energy in lockstep. Because you and all the other onlookers recognized a pattern as well, you began mentally chanting, as if back in grade school, "Fight! Fight! Fight! Fight!" Nobody wanted it to actually escalate to fisticuffs, but apparently everyone wanted a little office drama to talk about for the next couple of months: "Do you remember when Samantha and Karl had their crazy row in the breakroom?"

It's Either a Binary World, or It's Not

Just as our brains are tuned to recognize sensory patterns quickly so we can make sense of visual and auditory stimuli, we are also tuned to recognize another common pattern: "right" versus "wrong." We have held the concepts of "right" and "wrong" as foundational reality, but they are actually judgments of information based on our perceptions. Viewing right and wrong as judgments of information based on perception can be an extremely difficult concept for some people. Since we were children, many of us have concepts about what's right and what's wrong as foundational, carved-in-stone. We generally learn from older people to judge right from wrong. Some people learn to judge right from wrong by way of religion, parents, or community members. The key thing to understand is that even though the concepts of right and wrong are deep seated, they are judgments, nonetheless. AND, they are fluid.

Now before your torches and pitchforks come out, let me give you an example. My mother, grandmother, and aunt taught me from a very early age not to look inside a woman's purse. My brother and father reinforced this rule with the enthusiasm of people who had made the mistake of looking inside a woman's purse and only survived to tell the cautionary tale. Consequently, if a woman ever asked young Eric for something in her purse, I would always bring the purse, rather than looking in it. Every time I did this, an adult rewarded me with praise about how polite and respectful I was, validating the pattern I learned that it was "bad" and "wrong" to go inside a woman's purse. For me, it was not a judgment; it was a rule. It was a fact.

What if one day, I'm walking down the sidewalk and see a woman coming in the opposite direction. As I get about twenty feet away, I notice she starts flailing her arms wildly, then tries to run, and then falls down in dramatic fashion. As she falls, I watch her purse swing above her head and go flying in my direction, landing about halfway between us. I run to her to see if she needs help. When I get there, her left arm and entire face are extremely swollen. Before she passes out, she musters enough breath to push out a few words past her swelling vocal cords, "Bee. Epi. Purse." Adding up all the clues, I take that to mean she had been stung by a bee and has a severe bee allergy. At that moment, I realize the purse I just stepped over had a potentially life-saving dose of epinephrine. As this poor woman continues to swell, I quickly realize I have just a few options. I can look around for another woman to open the purse (because looking inside a woman's purse is wrong), or I can bring the purse to her and try to rouse her enough to get the EpiPen out of her purse. Or I can simply look in the purse, grab the epinephrine shot, and save this woman's life.

The solution to my hypothetical dilemma seems obvious (get in that purse and save her life!), but at that crucial moment, as a young boy, I could only look in her purse and save her life if I believe that I am either breaking a rule or that the rule is flexible given the context of an emergency. Either way, going inside her purse would be the right thing to do. Which means that what I believed as fact from listening to adults ("going inside of a woman's purse is wrong") was only their judgment based on their perception of particular situations or contexts. In sorting the world into right or wrong, good or bad, happy or sad, we are all making judgments like the one I would have had to make for that woman that day. Making judgments isn't necessarily wrong (you see what I did there?), but it's important to understand that the binaries of right and wrong are not concrete. In other words, given a different context, it's possible for a rule like, "It's wrong to look into a woman's purse" to be incorrect, even life-threatening.

Realizing these binary rules are not concrete is also the reason you can have an argument with someone and both of you believe that the other person is wrong. In such an argument, you know three things to be true: you are right, the other person is wrong, and you are rational. An easy conclusion surfaces when the other person tries to argue that they are right. They are irrational! "How could you possibly?" And, of course, that person is thinking the exact same thing about you—"You're irrational, you idiot." The thing is that in an argument, every single person fundamentally believes that they are rational. Let me repeat. Every single person that disagrees with you fundamentally believes that their opinion is rational. When you truly understand this concept, you will begin to listen to people differently. That is what our world needs. Less fighting and more understanding. Less debating and more solving.

When you comprehend The Trap of the Binary, the nineteenth Principle of Human Understanding, you see that rightness and wrongness depend on perception, experience, context, and a host of other factors. All of a sudden, it's much easier to understand another person's point of view.

JAMES' STORY

James woke up to sounds of muffled groaning. He wasn't sure how long he had been asleep or what time it was, but it was definitely still dark out. He rolled over to rub his wife's back and ask her how she was doing, but she wasn't there. "Kate?" he said into the blackness. Kate responded with a groan. She was sitting at the foot of the bed. After a few seconds, she let out a relieved breath. "I think we're getting close."

Kate and James had rehearsed for this moment every other day for the past month. James knew exactly what to do—consult his list:

~~Pack the hospital bag and load it into the truck~~ (Done last week)
Open the contraction timer app.
Measure a few contractions for duration and frequency.
Call the doctor.
Drive to the hospital.

James fumbles around and finds his phone on the night stand. He opens the contraction timer app and waits for the next contraction. It turns out that Kate's contractions were about 10 minutes apart, but they were growing in intensity. Yesterday, they were strong, but she could adjust her legs and eventually get herself back to sleep. These were different—they consumed her. The rest of the night, James and Kate breathed their way through contractions that got consistently more powerful and increasingly closer together but never hit the magic "go to the hospital" number that their doctor told them: "at least 45 seconds long and less than 5 minutes apart."

By sunrise the excitement of "we're in labor" was starting to fade. They understood that this was going to be a time to roll up their proverbial sleeves and work. James' thumbs and forearms ached from massaging Kate's lower back as she labored on the big blue yoga ball. Every muscle in Kate's body ached from the periodic involuntary intense spasm of her entire abdomen. Kate was telling James about her ideas for transforming the nursery as baby Marie reached various stages of life when, in an instant, a contraction washed over her that stopped the conversation in its tracks. This one was different from the rest. It was deeper, it was longer—the only word Kate could use to describe it was, "productive."

As the contraction released Kate to resume the nursery conversation, she looked up at James and realized that his mouth was agape. He was staring at the timer app. "That was 60 seconds, Kate! That was the longest one yet! You're doing great!" With a smile, she drew a deep breath and continued talking about toddler beds and wall decals, when another powerful contraction abruptly stopped the conversation. At this point, Kate was starting to get the hang of this. She could start to feel them coming and could go to her meditative place before the contraction took control. According to James' app, the next four contractions were spaced at 4.2 minutes, 5.5 minutes, 3.6 minutes, and 2.9 minutes. The adrenaline began flowing.

It was now time to load Kate into the truck, call the doctor, and get to the hospital. James and Kate completely forgot about the night of laboring as soon as James turned the key to start the engine because as he did, Kate turned to him and said, "Let's go become parents!"

James looked over his shoulder to the back seat to verify that the infant car seat was still properly installed. He had moved it a couple of times as they were loading some of what he called, "the nursery equipment." But everything was as it should be. Most importantly, the hospital bag with baby Marie's first outfit and other necessities was right behind his seat.

James pulled out of the garage onto their quarter-mile farm road driveway to get to the main road as another powerful contraction gripped Kate. Instinctively, Kate grabbed the door handle and James' right arm as she tried to slowly breathe her way through the contraction. The grip-strength Kate exhibited startled James. It was beyond anything he thought she was capable of, which made him realize they were probably closer to having the baby than he originally thought. They NEEDED to get to the hospital.

As the contraction subsided, James was relieved both by the blood returning to his right hand and because their pre-planned route to the hospital went down Orchard Road. Orchard Road was built extra-wide for tractors and farming equipment and had a speed limit of 50 miles per hour. "Good thing nobody ever takes Orchard this time of day," James thought.

As James turned the truck right onto Orchard Road, directly in front of them a man was driving a white sedan like it was Sunday morning. Completely oblivious to anything around him, the driver had his elbow poked so far out of the window, it looked like he was trying to fly. Without even trying, James found himself right up on the bumper of the sedan, which he could now see was a Toyota Camry. As James looked down, he realized his speedometer said the truck was going only 40 miles per hour. "C'mon c'mon," James thought out loud, "Can't you see the speed limit sign? We need to get to the hospital! How could you possibly be going this slow?!" Just then, James heard Kate say, "There's another one coming."

Usually a strictly by-the-book driver, James knew he needed to act or deliver the baby himself on the side of Orchard Road. As Kate's next contraction hit, James gently eased to the over-sized shoulder and accelerated past the Camry, waving his hand as if to say, "Sorry." As he pulled back into the normal lane of traffic, James locked his cruise control at 52 miles per hour and within three contractions, he and Kate were in the ER drop-off loop at the hospital. Their doctor met them with a nurse and a wheelchair, whisking Kate away to the labor and delivery floor. James parked the truck and thought about the inconsiderate Camry driver. His frustration was short-lived, however, because as soon as he got out of the truck and shut the door, he felt a wave of expectant excitement for the new life about to be welcomed into the world. He was going to be a dad.

Different Points of View, Different Conclusions

If you didn't pick up on it, James' Story and Paul's Story from Chapter 2 are the exact same sequence of events, just told from different perspectives. James and Paul both believed to their core that the other man was the one making life hard. Paul made James a villain and told everyone he could about the terrible driver who spewed black diesel smoke into his car. All he was trying to do was enjoy a beautiful day. James, on the other hand, believed that Paul was a terrible driver because he was going ten miles under the speed limit, slowing him and Kate down from getting to the hospital.

Similarly, when you get into arguments about who's right and who's wrong at work, remember that the other person is operating from a different set of beliefs than you. In your colleague's mind, she is entirely rational and correct, just as you believe that you are correct and rational. Whether the debate is about how to innovate a process or where to move corporate headquarters, you must understand and accept that people with a different point of view might know information or have context that you do not. They see the world differently from you. In this situation, we often oversimplify our thinking: "If you can't see the logic in my argument, then you're an idiot." This oversimplification is an illusion.

Cause and Effect Illusion

Most of us live our lives with the belief that reality is a series of causes and effects. Unfortunately, that's not actually the case. After reading the previous chapters, I hope that you have come to realize there are many more underlying inputs guiding our perceptions and behaviors than we typically take time to understand and accept. My mom says all the time, "Just like most diseases, life is multifactorial." Meaning we are complex beings, made up of many complex systems, and when those systems interact, the overall system (us) becomes exponentially more complex. It is erroneous, albeit common, to assume that one thing by itself causes another thing by itself. In fact, there are many, many factors that are all at play and ultimately produce some result.

An example of this complexity is a concept called the "Coastline Paradox."[47] According to nineteenth century mathematician Lewis Fry Richardson, if you are trying to measure the length of shoreline of an island using Google Maps or some other cartography software, getting an accurate measure will prove impossibly difficult. After you take your first measurement, you could zoom in on the map, revealing more shoreline detail. If you measured again at that higher resolution, your measurement would be nowhere close to your first one. After that, you could zoom in yet again and get an even higher measurement.

You can see this yourself by using Google Maps' measure distance feature. The measure feature allows you to click two points on a map and the distance between those two points will be displayed. If you click more points, creating more line segments, the total distance will be displayed. All you need to do is go to Google Maps and find an island (or a lake for that matter) and right-click anywhere on the map. In the context menu that pops up, find the option for "measure distance."

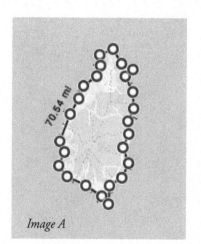

Image A

Then click point by point, following the shoreline. When you make it all the way around, note the total distance, zoom in and measure it again.

Here's an example from St. Lucia, an island in the Caribbean. When I go around the island using the measurement tool, I get a total perimeter distance of 70.54 miles (113.53 km). You can see the measurement in image A.

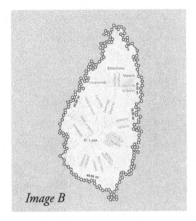

Image B

The second time that I measured the island, I zoomed in about six times closer, making more land feature detail visible. You can see the measurement in image B. When I went around the island with the tool, I clicked significantly more line segments and I got a total distance of 98.87 miles (159.12 km).

The second measurement was 26 percent larger! If I were to zoom in even farther, the measurement would get larger. This measurement paradox continues even when you get down to the level of the moving water or individual grains of sand. According to Richardson, there are virtually infinite "accurate" measurements of a coastline, even though the actual coastline is fixed.

This same Coastline Paradox concept is true when we are trying to identify the cause or causes of an outcome in our environment, either at home or at work. Our natural reaction is to believe that there was one thing that caused one other thing. This is the Cause and Effect Illusion, the twentieth Principle of Human Understanding. The reality of life, however, is just like the Coastline Paradox—the closer you look at an issue, the more details or factors you will be able to attribute as causes. Most issues are multifactorial. In other words, the closer you look at a situation between coworkers, for example, the more you discover there is more to learn—even though the Illusion of Certainty is trying to convince you that you have already assessed the situation accurately.

In the break room, as Karl continued to yell and his hands continued to flail, Samantha suddenly realized she wasn't thinking about the problem. She had her next sentence locked and loaded, just waiting for the right break to insert her comment into the conversation. All of a sudden, she realized she was trying to win. She also realized that Karl wasn't trying to solve the problem either. He was trying not to lose. He was playing defense. "Why would

Karl be defensive right now?" she thought. "He's the one being aggressive with me." She zoomed in and realized that if he was defensive, he must feel like she was attacking him.

Samantha put both of her hands up, palms facing Karl, and took a step back. The action Samantha took was so far outside the expected pattern of behavior that it took Karl by surprise. Confused, he stopped right in the middle of his sentence, still breathing heavily with one cleaver hand slowly going back down to his side.

Samantha looked Karl in the eye and, rather than tell him more of her opinions, she asked him a question. "Karl, why do you feel so strongly about this sign?" Still not sure what was going on, Karl picked up his intensity where he left off, hands waving. "You people don't respect me and understand how much I do for the entire office. All you want to do is leave a mess. KARL will clean it up for you! I've had enough!"

Even though the phrase, "you people" stung, Samantha intentionally avoided FAE and assumed that Karl meant "you night-shift people." She didn't rebuke him. She didn't argue. She simply asked him a follow up question. "Karl, when I come in to the office, it's hours after you do. Please forgive me. I have no idea what you mean when you say that you do so much for the entire office." Once again, Karl felt caught off guard.

Now you and the other people who have been attracted to this public argument are leaning in with curiosity. Karl responded with a calmer voice, but still with a hint of skepticism: "Well, I'm usually the first one in every morning. I'm the one who starts the coffee every morning, the coffee that everyone drinks." And as he said this, he began to get animated again. "And nobody understands what I do. They leave stale coffee in the pot on all night, and I have to scrub it in the morning. I hate scrubbing coffee stains! The least you could do is clean it in the afternoon. Why should I have to do both jobs?"

Then the distinction became clear to Samantha. She was certain that Karl was selfish and inconsiderate, but by listening and letting go of the Fight for Right, she realized that Karl really wanted to be understood and appreciated. His logic was based in rational thought. Karl believed that he was doing a service for the people in the office, but he didn't feel like the people in the office were respecting him. The sign Karl hung, which still offended Samantha, was a reaction to his feeling of frustration. Samantha realized that for the majority of their interaction, she had attributed Karl's behavior to the fact that he was irrational. She judged that he was stupid. When she actually stopped to listen to the meaning behind Karl's argument, she saw that given his perspective, his frustration was reasonable. She didn't necessarily agree with it, nor would she have reacted the same way, but she understood.

Samantha then did something powerful. She looked Karl in the eye and said to him, "I'm sorry, Karl. I had no idea that it was you who made the coffee in the morning. Because I come in so late, it's always hot and ready when I get here. I guess I've never even considered the idea that someone made it in the morning. Thank you for doing that every day." Her genuine apology evaporated all the tension between them. Karl's shoulders lowered. He calmed down. "Thank you," he said. "But you know something, I never asked you why you were so upset, Samantha."

As you've been reading this book looking for the cure for stupidity, I hope you now realize that we humans are very complex organisms—a combination of all our thoughts, experiences, and biology. Whenever you interact with your spouse, your family, your co-workers, and even with strangers at the mall, people will inevitably behave in some irrational way. When that happens, it's my hope that you realize that you have been granted the opportunity to understand them rather than judge them critically. With the Principles of Human Understanding, you are now armed with the tools to cure stupidity.

Principles of Human Understanding

The Observation Trap Principles

Can trap us by influencing the way we observe the world.

1. The Illusion of Certainty
2. Perception is More Important Than Reality
3. The Desire to Fight to Be Right
4. The Power of Distinction
5. Context is the Underlying Fabric by Which We Encounter the World
6. Empathy Changes Your Judgment

The Orientation Trap Principles

Can trap us by augmenting how we orient ourselves in the world.

7. The Truth About Bias
8. Understanding Fundamental Attribution Error (FAE)
9. The Insidious Nature of Joy from Pain
10. The Fluidity of Tribal Boundaries
11. The Validation of Truth

The Decision Trap Principles

Can trap us by leading us to make uninformed decisions.

12. The Truth About Judgment / Decisions
13. Just OODA It!
14. Cognitive Destruction from Distraction
15. Mutual Purpose, The Solution for Debate
16. The Myth of Multitasking
17. Stereotype Expectations

The Action Trap Principles

Can trap us by leading us to take the wrong action.

18. The Pull of Patterns
19. The Trap of Binary
20. Cause and Effect Illusion

Check Your Blind Spot

"What is necessary to change a person
is to change his awareness of himself."

—Abraham Maslow

In addition to all the other principles discussed in this book, the "Bias Blind Spot" can show us the most about ourselves. According to the APA Dictionary, Bias Blind Spot is similar to Fundamental Attribution Error, in which we see things in other people differently from how we see them in ourselves. Specifically, the Bias Blind Spot demonstrates that we will clearly see the biases (systematic errors in thinking) in other people and fail to see the biases in ourselves. Said another way, "Lord, give me the strength to forgive those who sin differently than I do."

When we go through a training or read a book of this nature, we tend to create a running list of other people who we think need this information. Those people might include your spouse, a boss, a cousin, or that overly entitled kid who served you at a restaurant. Sharing this book with that list of people will help our mission of changing the way the world communicates. But more importantly, this twenty-first Principle of Human Understanding, the Bias Blind Spot, will help you realize that as certain as you are that people on your Bias Blind Spot List need to read this book, you, too, are definitely on somebody else's Bias Blind Spot List. And I am too!

As you know by now, I'm an expert in the Principles of Human

Understanding. I literally wrote the book on them. Even though I travel around the world teaching these concepts, I can say without hesitation that I am on my wife's Bias Blind Spot List. No matter how good we are at communicating, there are always things we can do as a couple to improve our relationship and our communication skills. The Illusion of Certainty is more powerful than you know, and what's worse? The more intelligent you believe you are, the stronger the grasp the Illusion of Certainty has on you.

I invite you to read through this book again and again. Understand that it's natural to see all these concepts, barriers, and fallacies through the lens of how other people fail. The Bias Blind Spot List reminds us to turn the lens inward, looking to see how we have room to improve. I subtitled this book, "Using Brain Science to Predict Irrational Behavior at Work," but I hope by now I've made it clear that the cure for stupidity is not in curing others, but rather, in curing ourselves and the ways that we perceive others. In short, the cure for stupidity lies within each of us.

You See?

I hope you have found this an information-rich book, but I do not operate under the delusion that you are going to take in all the information after reading it once and become a master of the Illusion of Certainty or the Perception Escalator and all the other Principles of Human Understanding. What I do hope, however, is that you gain some awareness about these concepts and how they impact your life and your relationships daily. Awareness of the world around you is powerful. Just as we discussed with The Power of Distinction, the OODA Loop, and the Conscious Competence Matrix earlier, awareness can change the way you see the world, giving you the opportunity to behave differently in it.

To help illustrate the power of awareness, look at the following photograph. Within this photograph, there is something hiding. As soon as you see this common object, it will appear completely unambiguous. Many people, when they first look at this image, think they see something, and their brain identifies what that thing might be because human beings like to see patterns.

When you think you have the image (or if you give up), just turn the page.

A CIGAR! Right smack in the middle of the wall. Now I want you to flip back to the first photograph, where you couldn't see it. This is the Power of Awareness and my final Principle of Human Understanding: Once You See It, You Can Never Not See It.

After reading *The Cure for Stupidity*, you now have awareness about many of the barriers to communication that plague organizations and relationships around the world. You're going to see these barriers pop up all the time. Whenever they do, rather than ask, "How could you possibly...?" what if you used your newfound knowledge of how our brains work to understand human beings' irrational behavior? If you continually learn and explore the Principles of Human Understanding, then instead of being annoyed, frustrated, or offended by other people's irrational behavior, you will more likely be able to offer coworkers, friends, and family compassion and understanding. And instead of seeing other people as irrational or stupid, you will more likely be able to see them as fallible human beings, worthy of respect and kindness—just like yourself.

Principles of Human Understanding

The Observation Trap Principles

Can trap us by influencing the way we observe the world.

1. The Illusion of Certainty
2. Perception is More Important Than Reality
3. The Desire to Fight to Be Right
4. The Power of Distinction
5. Context is the Underlying Fabric by Which We Encounter the World
6. Empathy Changes Your Judgment

The Orientation Trap Principles

Can trap us by augmenting how we orient ourselves in the world.

7. The Truth About Bias
8. Understanding Fundamental Attribution Error (FAE)
9. The Insidious Nature of Joy from Pain
10. The Fluidity of Tribal Boundaries
11. The Validation of Truth

The Decision Trap Principles

Can trap us by leading us to make uninformed decisions.

12. The Truth About Judgment / Decisions
13. Just OODA It!
14. Cognitive Destruction from Distraction
15. Mutual Purpose, The Solution for Debate
16. The Myth of Multitasking
17. Stereotype Expectations

The Action Trap Principles

Can trap us by leading us to take the wrong action.

18. The Pull of Patterns
19. The Trap of Binary
20. Cause and Effect Illusion
21. The Blind Spot List
22. The Power of Awareness

Notes

1 Daniel J. Boorstin, *Hidden History: Exploring Our Secret Past* (New York: Harper and Row, 1987).

2 Jacques Ninio and Stevens, Kent, "Variations on the Hermann Grid: An Extinction Illusion," *Perception* 29, no. 10, (2000),1209-17.

3 Charles G. Lord, Lee Ross, and Mark R. Lepper, "Biased Assimilation and Attitude Polarization: The Effects of Prior Theories on Subsequently Considered Evidence," *Journal of Personality and Social Psychology*, 37, no. 11, 1979, 2098-2019, http://fbaum.unc.edu/teaching/articles/jpsp-1979-Lord-Ross-Lepper.pdf.

4 Douglas Stone and Sheila Heen, *Thanks for the Feedback: The Science and Art of Receiving Feedback Well* (New York: Penguin Books, 2015), 102.

5 Guy Deutscher, *Through the Language Glass: Why the World Looks Different in Other Languages* (Henry Holt and Company, 2010), 71-72.

6 William Ewart Gladstone, *Studies on Homer and the Homeric Age* (Oxford: Oxford University Press, 1858), 456.

7 Debi Roberson, Jules B. Davidoff, Ian R. L. Davies, and Laura R. Shapiro, "Color Categories: Evidence for the Cultural Relativity Hypothesis," *Cognitive Psychology* 50, no. 4, (2005), 378-411.

8 Kerry Patterson, Joseph Grenny, Ron McMillan, and Al Switzler, *Crucial Conversations: Tools for Talking When Stakes Are High* (New York: McGraw-Hill, 2012).

9 Ibid. 24-28

10 PR Newswire, "Living Paycheck to Paycheck is a Way of Life for Majority of U.S. Workers, According to New CareerBuilder Survey," http://press.careerbuilder.com/2017-08-24-Living-Paycheck-to-Paycheck-is-a-Way-of-Life-for-Majority-of-U-S-Workers-According-to-New-CareerBuilder-Survey.

11 Steve Siebold, *How Rich People Think* (London: London House Press, 2010).

12 Jill E. P. Knapen, Nancy M. Blaker, and Mark Van Vugt, "The Napoleon Complex: When Shorter Men Take More," *Psychological Science* 29, no.7, (2018).

13 Dr. Matt Grawitch, "Oh, No, Say It Aint So—There's no Evidence for Engagement Alarmism?" Good Company Blog (June 5, 2017), http://www.apaexcellence.org/resources/goodcompany/blog/2017/06/engagement-alarmism-hype.php.

14 Raymond B. Cattell. *Intelligence: Its Structure, Growth, and Action* (New York: Elsevier, 1987).

15 "Understanding the Stress Response: Chronic activation of this survival mechanism impairs health," *Harvard Health Publishing, Harvard Medical School,* https://www.health.harvard.edu/staying-healthy/understanding-the-stress-response.

16 "Defense Mechanism," APA Dictionary of Psychology, American Psychological Association, https://dictionary.apa.org/defense-mechanism.

17 Kendra Cherry, "How Cognitive Biases Influence How You Think and Act," *Very Well Mind,* https://www.verywellmind.com/what-is-a-cognitive-bias-2794963.

18 "Fundamental Attribution Error," APA Dictionary of Psychology, *American Psychological Association,* https://dictionary.apa.org/fundamental-attribution-error.

19 "Professionally Active Physicians by Gender," Henry J. Kaiser Family Foundation, https://www.kff.org/other/state-indicator/physicians-by-gender/?currentTimeframe=0&sortModel=%7B%22colId%22:%22Locatio n%22,%22sort%22:%22asc%22%7D.

20 Paul James, *Globalism, Nationalism, Tribalism: Bringing Theory Back In* (Thousand Oaks: SAGE Publications, Inc., 2006), 330.

21 "World Population Prospects 2017," United Nations DESA/Population Division, https://population.un.org/wpp/DataQuery/.

22 John T. Jones, Brett W. Pelham, and Mauricio Carvallo, "How Do I Love Thee? Let Me Count the Js: Implicit Egotism and Interpersonal Attraction," *Journal of Personality and Social Psychology*, 87, no. 5, 2004: 665–683.

23 Adam L. Alter and Daniel M. Oppenheimer, "Uniting the Tribes of Fluency to Form a Metacognitive Nation" *Personality and Social Psychology Review* 13, no. 3 (July 28, 2009): 219-235.

24 John R. Boyd, *The Essence of Winning and Losing*, Chet Richards and Chuck Spinney, eds., (September 2012): https://fasttransients.files. wordpress.com/2010/03/essence_of_winning_losing.pdf

25 Myles Keating, "Innovate presents Barry McCarthy, Chief Financial Officer of Netflix," *The Unofficial Stanford Blog*, http://tusb.stanford. edu/2008/01/barry_mccarthy_chief_financial.html.

26 Tony Robbins, *Awaken the Giant Within* (New York: Simon and Schuster, 2012) 56.

27 Susan Cain, *Quiet: The Power of Introverts in a World That Won't Stop Talking* (Massachusets: Crown Publishing, 2012), 74.

28 Adrian F. Ward, Kristen Duke, Ayelet Gneezy, and Maarten W. Bos, "Brain Drain: The Mere Presence of One's Own Smartphone Reduces Available Cognitive Capacity," *Journal of the Association of Consumer Research*, 2, no. 2, 2017: 143.

29 World Wide Web Timeline, Pew Research Center, https://www. pewinternet.org/2014/03/11/world-wide-web-timeline/.

30 Simon Sinek, *Start with Why: How Great Leaders Inspire Everyone to Take Action* (New York: Penguin 2009), 41.

31 Alison Overholt, "The Art of Multitasking," *Fast Company*, September 30, 2002, https://www.fastcompany.com/45388/art-multitasking.

32 Robert D. Rogers and Stephen Monsell, "Costs of a Predictable Switch between Simple Cognitive Tasks," *Journal of Experimental Psychology: General* 124, 2, June 1995: 207-231 https://psycnet.apa.org/buy/1995-31890-001.

33 Jim Taylor, PhD, "Technology: Myth of Multitasking," *Psychology Today*, March 30, 2011, https://www.psychologytoday.com/us/blog/the-power-prime/201103/technology-myth-multitasking,

34 Art Markman, "Sorry, But Your Brain Only Knows One Way to Multitask Effectively," *Fast Company*, January 18, 2017, https://www.fastcompany. com/3067257/sorry-but-your-brain-only-knows-one-way-to-multitask-effectively.

35 Martin Broadwell, "Teaching for Learning (XVI)," *The Gospel Guardian* 20, no. 41, February 20, 1969: 1.

36 A. N. Kluger and A. DeNisi, "The Effects of Feedback Interventions on Performance: A Historical Review, a Meta-analysis, and a Preliminary Feedback Intervention Theory," *Psychological Bulletin*, 119, no. 2, 1996: 254-284.

37 S. L. Beilock, R. J. Rydell, and A. R. McConnell, "Stereotype Threat and Working Memory: Mechanisms, Alleviation, and Spillover," *Journal of Experimental Psychology: General* 136, no. 2, 2007: 256-276.

38 Gregory M. Walton, Christine Logel, Jennifer M. Peach, Steven J. Spencer and Mark P. Zanna, "Two Brief Interventions to Mitigate a "Chilly Climate" Transform Women's Experience, Relationships, and Achievement in Engineering," *Journal of Educational Psychology* 107, no. 2, 2015: 468-485.

39 S. L. Beilock, R. J. Rydell, & A. R. McConnell, "Stereotype Threat and Working Memory: Mechanisms, Alleviation, and Spillover," *Journal of Experimental Psychology: General* 136, no. 2, 2007: 256-276.

40 Tup Wanders, https://www.flickr.com/photos/tupwanders/3723200395/, CC BY 2.0.

41 Mikel Ortega, https://www.flickr.com/photos/mikelo/21119314498, CC BY-SA 2.0.

42 Trevor Hurlbut, https://www.flickr.com/photos/hurtre/4689253598, CC BY 2.0.

43 Karen Mardahl, https://www.flickr.com/photos/kmardahl/18170822588, CC BY-SA 2.0.

44 Berthold Werner, https://commons.wikimedia.org/wiki/File:Austin-Healey_Sprite_AN5_Mark_I_Frogeye_2012-07-15_13-58-32.JPG, CC BY-SA 3.0.

45 Procsilas Moscas, https://commons.wikimedia.org/wiki/File:Pareidolia_(15468122).jpg, CC BY 2.0.

46 "Gambler's Fallacy," *APA Dictionary of Psychology*, https://dictionary.apa.org/gamblers-fallacy.

47 L. B. Richardson, *Collected Papers of Lewis Frye Richardson* (New York: Cambridge University Press, 1993), 45.

Acknowledgments

The development of this book could not have been done without the help and guidance from my large tribe.

Family

I have been fortunate to live an amazing life. I have experienced things (both good and bad) that most people haven't. I have been given opportunities that I did nothing to deserve. I am living my great grandparent's wildest dreams. Thank you to my large, brilliant, beautiful family. You have all given me so much guidance and opportunity to be confident enough to write this book. Since I'm at risk of adding another chapter of the book just for listing my family, I will only list a few.

To my mom, Rose, who taught me to never give up and encouraged me to be a big fish in a big pond.

To my wife, Jamie, my peace and my balance.

To my kids, Jarem, Kai, and Jasmine, thank you for keeping my heart full of love.

To my brother Kenn, who has always protected me and taught me how to survive and thrive.

To my dad, Kenn, who taught me how deep human love and forgiveness can go.

To my brother, Mica, who influenced my success ;-).

To my stepdad, Gary, who introduced me to a world filled with things that I didn't know.

To my aunt Linda, if her heart was literally made of gold, she would find a way to share it.

To my cousin Troy, my example of what a man can be when he lives a life for others.

To my aunt Lola, who saw something special in me and never quit telling me until I believed her. . . and when I finally did, she kept on telling me.

To my cousin Kacia, you will always be my "hart," and I will always be your "hutt."

To my cousin Monika, thank you for teaching me to Hold The Line.

To my mother-in-law, Karla, thank you for your relentless optimism no matter what life brings.

To my father-in-law, Roby, the epitome of relentless hard work to get a project done.

To all of my family that can no longer share family dinners or picnics: my Grandma and Grandpa Ford, Uncle Tommy, Pop Pop and so many others. Thank you for laying the foundation, giving me the tools, and wishing for me to shine. I hope every day that I make you proud.

Friends

I have been blessed with a powerful extension of my family in numerous friends that have shaped the person I have become. They have willingly been part of the highs and the lows of my life to give me guidance, support, and critical feedback when necessary. Thank you to each of my friends, especially . . .

To Niki, my best friend and business partner, who taught me how time works and how to practice what I preach.

To Seth, whose gentle approach to influencing people changed the way I saw power.

To Megan, the confidence booster who has, without fail, lifted me up with every single conversation we've had.

To MacKenna, it turns out I am a Bold Egg!

To H, "It wasn't ideal, but if we made it through that, we can do anything!"

To all my friends near and far, thank you for always making me smile.

Mentors

Writing this book has been a decades long dream, but thanks to the support and encouragement from a group of mentors, I was actually able to "write my damn book."

To Cynthia Nustadt, who was so confident that I could write this book, I started drafting it right after a breakfast meeting with her.

To Simon Bailey, my "cousin" who is a shining example of what is possible.

To Tiana Sanchez, who paved the way and showed me *The Upside of Failure*.

To Tana Session, who let me know that writing my book was not only possible, but necessary.

To Dr. Laura Bush, who stuck with me for nearly a decade knowing that I had a book in me; she was right!

To Jennifer Lawrence, the Logistics Ninja who kept me on time, on task, and on message.

To Scott Grondin, my first leader, thank you for seeing my unique ability and allowing me to explore the realm of possibility.

To Dr. Randy Currier, who miraculously shaped a lump of clay into a sculpture of a bird and let that bird fly.

To Dennis Goin, thank you for accelerating my career by showing me that consulting can be done differently.

To Dr. John P. Kotter, who opened my eyes to a new level of comprehending the world.

To Dr. Steve Winton, who showed me unexpected kindness at Saint Louis University and lit a fire of curiosity for the world of Organizational Development.

To Fr. Jerry Chapdelaine, my first football coach, who showed me that there is no actual limit to happiness and kindness.

Book Support Team

So many colleagues joined the effort to spread the word about *The Cure for Stupidity*. Whether it was their curiosity about the title or their desire to spread the message, this group of people boldly shared the message, helping me and my book reach a vastly larger audience than I could have done myself. To every member of the team, thank you.

Clients and Partners

I spend most of my time working with clients and partners all over the world. People share their stories and tell me how my words have influenced their life. I have found so much encouragement from our client partners that many of them have become friends. It was in response to their urging that I started laying out the manuscript of *The Cure for Stupidity*. Thank you. I hope you enjoyed it!

About the Author

Eric M. Bailey, President of Bailey Strategic Innovation Group, leads one of the fastest-growing communication consulting firms in the United States. His unique style blends fact and emotion, enabling him to appeal to analytical thinkers, emotional feelers, and everyone in between. He has helped an NFL player pet a rhinoceros, done barrel rolls in an F-16, and chatted with LL Cool J on the campus of Harvard University. He has also helped leaders and teams across North America see common problems from new and different perspectives.

With a master's degree in Leadership and Organizational Development from Saint Louis University, Eric is a lifelong learner of human and organizational behavior. He consults with Google Inc., the US Air Force, Los Angeles County, Phoenix PD, and many others around the world. He has been featured in the Huffington Post, Forbes, and the Like a Real Boss Podcast.

When not working or researching, you can find Eric and his wife, Jamie, racing their road bikes, cheered on by their three children.

If you want to learn more about how to leverage *The Cure for Stupidity* in your organization, please contact Eric M. Bailey.

Website: www.EricMBailey.com
LinkedIn: www.Linkedin.com/in/EricMBailey
Twitter: @Eric_M_Bailey
Instagram: @Eric_M_Bailey

Made in USA - North Chelmsford, MA
1266040_9781732242784
02.24.2023 2206